By Meghan Green

Portions of this book originally appeared in *Abortion* by Wendy Lanier.

PRESS

Published in 2018 by
Lucent Press, an Imprint of Greenhaven Publishing, LLC
353 3rd Avenue
Suite 255
New York, NY 10010

Designer: Seth Hughes
Editor: Jennifer Lombardo

Library of Congress Cataloging-in-Publication Data

Names: Green, Meghan, author.
Title: Abortion : a continuing debate / by Meghan Green.
Description: New York : Lucent Press, 2018. | Series: Hot topics | Includes
    bibliographical references and index.
Identifiers: LCCN 2017035230| ISBN 9781534561977 (library bound book) | ISBN
    9781534562882 (paperback)
Subjects: LCSH: Abortion–Juvenile literature. | Abortion–Moral and ethical
    aspects.
Classification: LCC HQ767 .G6827 2018 | DDC 179.7/6–dc23
LC record available at https://lccn.loc.gov/2017035230

CPSIA compliance information: Batch #CW18KL: For further information contact Greenhaven Publishing LLC, New York,
New York at 1-844-317-7404.

Please visit our website, www.greenhavenpublishing.com. For a free color catalog of all our
high-quality books, call toll free 1-844-317-7404 or fax 1-844-317-7405.

CONTENTS

Adolescence is a time when many people begin to take notice of the world around them. News channels, blogs, and talk radio shows are constantly promoting one view or another; very few are unbiased. Young people also hear conflicting information from parents, friends, teachers, and acquaintances. Often, they will hear only one side of an issue or be given flawed information. People who are trying to support a particular viewpoint may cite inaccurate facts and statistics on their blogs, and news programs present many conflicting views of important issues in our society. In a world where it seems everyone has a platform to share their thoughts, it can be difficult to find unbiased, accurate information about important issues.

It is not only facts that are important. In blog posts, in comments on online videos, and on talk shows, people will share opinions that are not necessarily true or false, but can still have a strong impact. For example, many young people struggle with their body image. Seeing or hearing negative comments about particular body types online can have a huge effect on the way someone views himself or herself and may lead to depression and anxiety. Although it is important not to keep information hidden from young people under the guise of protecting them, it is equally important to offer encouragement on issues that affect their mental health.

The titles in the Hot Topics series provide readers with different viewpoints on important issues in today's society. Many of these issues, such as teen pregnancy and Internet safety, are of immediate concern to young people. This series aims to give readers factual context on these crucial topics in a way that lets them form their own opinions. The facts presented throughout also serve to empower readers to help themselves or support people they know who are struggling with many of the challenges adolescents face today. Although negative viewpoints are not ignored or downplayed, this series allows young people to see that the challenges they face are not insurmountable. Eating disorders can be overcome, the Internet can be navigated safely, and pregnant teens do not have to feel hopeless.

Quotes encompassing all viewpoints are presented and cited so readers can trace them back to their original source, verifying for themselves whether the information comes from a reputable place. Additional books and websites are listed, giving readers a starting point from which to continue their own research. Chapter questions encourage discussion, allowing young people to hear and understand their classmates' points of view as they further solidify their own. Full-color photographs and enlightening charts provide a deeper understanding of the topics at hand. All of these features augment the informative text, helping young people understand the world they live in and formulate their own opinions concerning the best way they can improve it.

A Long History of Controversy

Abortion has been one of the most controversial topics in American politics for many years. Some people believe it is morally wrong to make it legal, while others believe just as firmly that it is irresponsible to make it illegal. The issue is complex and involves many factors. Because these factors are different for every woman, people who call themselves pro-choice believe a woman should be allowed to consider all the factors and make the choice that is best for her. On the other hand, people who call themselves pro-life believe none of these factors matter when the life of a fetus is at stake. However, there is no possible way to say that every single person who is pro-life or pro-choice believes a particular thing. With so many issues to consider, even multiple people who use the same label will likely differ on at least one point.

Abortion was illegal in most states until 1973, when the Supreme Court decided in the now-famous *Roe v. Wade* case that preventing early-term abortion was unconstitutional. This decision paved the way for legal abortions and unleashed a firestorm of controversy over moral and legal obligations to women and unborn children.

For the past several decades, people on both sides of the issue have continued to debate the question of whether legal abortions should be made available to women and to what point in their pregnancy. At times the debate has turned violent. Angry clashes between pro-life and pro-choice demonstrators have resulted in property damage, fights, abortion clinic bombings, and even murder. Feelings run high among extremists on both sides.

Now, in the 21st century, the questions remain. There is no one pro-life or pro-choice position. Different terms have different definitions among different groups. New technology has made earlier detection of pregnancy possible. At the same time, new options for early abortions have become available. These factors have ultimately created more questions without providing any answers.

Protests connected with legal abortion are common on both sides of the issue.

Although the *Roe v. Wade* Supreme Court decision of 1973 made abortion legal, later court cases gave states the right to regulate certain things, such as deciding the cutoff point for having a legal abortion and placing restrictions on abortion facilities. Because of this, abortion access varies greatly from state to state. Some states require parental notification or permission for minors, while others do not. Many have varying amounts of mandatory counseling prior to abortion services as well as a specified waiting period. Some states allow late-term abortions, while others have strict limits on abortions after certain points in the pregnancy.

Since the U.S. Supreme Court's *Roe v. Wade* decision, there have been many attempts to pass laws regulating abortion access. Political groups on both sides of the abortion issue have established powerful lobbies—groups of people who try to convince politicians to vote a certain way on specific laws—in an effort to influence the outcome of elections. Political candidates find the question of abortion to be a minefield they sometimes try to avoid. At times the outcome of an election has been determined by a candidate's stance on this one issue.

The questions surrounding the abortion issue are many and complex. Is abortion a moral solution to an unintended pregnancy? What right, if any, does the government or anyone else have to limit abortion access to a woman who is pregnant? How much power should states have to limit access to abortion? Should men be allowed to make laws regulating abortion without consulting women? These and many other questions continue to be debated both in public and in private.

A Debate About Morality

One of the biggest reasons why people who are pro-life support making abortion illegal is because they believe it is immoral. Morality is a complex and often confusing subject. It refers to standards of what is good and bad behavior; something moral is good or righteous, and something immoral is bad or evil. Every person has their own idea of morality, which is generally influenced by their life experiences. For instance, one person may think abortion is immoral, while someone else who has had different life experiences may think there is nothing wrong with it.

There are no real absolutes in a discussion about morality. It cannot be said that all members of a certain group of people feel a certain way. A person's view of morality depends on the way they were raised, their personal experiences, the movies they watch and books they read, who they are friends with, their religious beliefs, and many other factors. Additionally, ideas about morality can change over time. Someone who thinks abortion is immoral when they are young may learn more about why abortions are performed, make friends with people who have had an abortion, and gradually come to the conclusion that abortion is not immoral after all. The reverse can also happen, although it is somewhat less common.

Just because someone does not think something is immoral does not necessarily mean they think it is the morally correct choice. Many people who are pro-choice do not generally assign a particular moral value to abortion. They feel a pregnant woman should be able to decide which choice best lines up with her own morals and situation, and if she decides to have an abortion, she should be allowed to do so. Other pro-choice people believe abortion is a moral option in certain situations, such as if the mother would be unable to properly care for her child.

In giving careful thought to the morality of abortion, two additional questions are often raised: At what point does life begin, and at what point do the rights of this developing life (if ever) overrule the rights of the mother? The answers have produced a range of feelings on the issue.

WHEN CAN A FETUS THINK?

"If we're talking about life in the biological sense, eggs are alive, sperm are alive. Cancer tumors are alive. For me, what matters is this: When does it have the moral status of a human being? When does it have some kind of awareness of its surroundings?"

—Bonnie Steinbock, professor of bioethics and philosophy

Quoted in "When Does Human Personhood Begin?," ReligiousTolerance.org, August 22, 2012. www.religioustolerance.org/abo_argu.htm.

Choosing Life

Most pro-life groups and many conservative Christians believe life begins at conception, which is when a woman's egg, or ovum, is fertilized by a man's sperm. At this point, the ovum is called a zygote. It contains 46 chromosomes in a DNA structure different from either the sperm or ovum that joined to create it. People who believe that abortion is immoral in all or most cases argue that a zygote is a new and unique human life with all the rights of any other human. In support of this view, physiologist Albert W. Liley observed, "Biologically, at no stage of development can we subscribe to the view that the unborn child is a mere appendage of the mother. Genetically, the mother and baby are separate individuals from conception."[1]

Those who view human life as beginning at conception give the same value to a zygote as they would a newborn. Any effort to prevent further development of the zygote to the pre-embryo stage—that is, before the zygote has divided into two cells—is viewed by them as the destruction of human life. Some believe even the use of emergency contraception, such as the Plan B pill, counts as a form of abortion. Plan B and other emergency contraception pills are medications a woman can take within 24 hours of having sex to try to prevent pregnancy. In most cases, the pill prevents the egg from being fertilized at all, so even by the strictest standards of when life begins, no abortion is taking place. Since fertilization is a process that takes place over several hours or even days, Plan B has a good chance of preventing fertilization if it is taken as soon as possible. However, people who consider emergency contraception to be abortion argue that it is impossible to know whether the pill is preventing fertilization in the first place or simply preventing the fertilized egg from implanting to the wall of the uterus, which is the moment at which a woman is considered pregnant. If the embryo does not implant into the uterine wall, pregnancy cannot occur, and the embryo will exit the woman's body when she gets her period.

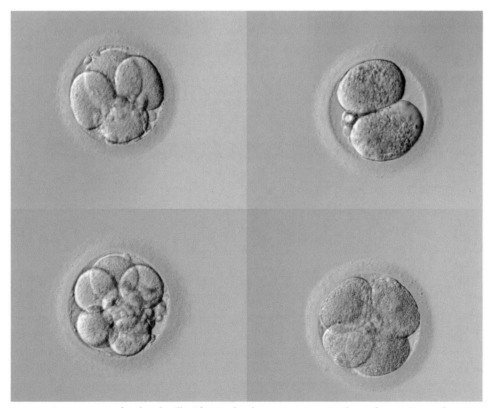

A zygote is a fertilized cell. After it divides once, it enters the embryonic period (shown here), which has multiple phases. After the eighth week of pregnancy, the term "fetus" is used.

Again, the morality of this issue is complex. Some people who call themselves pro-life may believe the zygote cannot be considered alive until it becomes an embryo and attaches to the uterine wall; others may believe it is alive as soon as the sperm fertilizes the egg. Others may have varying opinions about when life begins. For instance, some people believe life truly begins when the baby's heartbeat can be detected. Since 2011, 14 states have proposed laws outlawing abortion after this point, which is generally about 4 to 6 weeks after conception. Many pro-choice advocates oppose these bills because sometimes a woman does not even know she is pregnant at this point. By the time she found out, it would be too late for her to decide whether or not she wanted an abortion.

ONE OPINION ON IMMORALITY

"Legality is not morality … It has been legal to murder an unborn baby in America for the last 30 years … But morality is eternal, and regardless of the current state of the law, such actions will always be immoral."

–Vox Day, author and opinion columnist

Vox Day, "R.I.P Connor Peterson," WorldNetDaily, April 28, 2003. www.wnd.com/news/article. asp?ARTICLE_ID=32267.

In general, pro-life advocates believe abortion is wrong even if the pregnancy is not wanted or the mother is uncertain of her ability to care for a child. In their view, the government should require a woman to continue her pregnancy to childbirth in many or all cases, with few exceptions.

Is Abortion Sometimes Justified?

Many Americans believe abortion is acceptable in some circumstances. Polls over the past decade show many people, including some pro-life supporters, do not believe a woman should have to endure any pregnancy caused by rape or incest, which is sexual intercourse between two people who are too closely related to legally marry. In addition, it is generally believed that a pregnancy that endangers the life or long-term health of the mother should be terminated. A 2017 report by the Pew Research Center indicated 24 percent of Americans believe abortions should be legal only under special circumstances such as these, compared to 16 percent who believe abortion should never be legal and 25 percent who believe it should always be legal. Because they believe these circumstances are beyond a woman's control, most people believe abortion is a moral option in these cases.

Some pro-life supporters are willing to make allowances for these special circumstances because they believe them to be rare. Research suggests such circumstances occur less than 7 percent of the time. In the pro-life view, only a small fraction of the abortions carried out in the United States each year are for acceptable reasons.

However, other pro-life supporters believe even rape and incest are not acceptable reasons for someone to have an abortion. They feel it is not the child's fault that it was conceived against the mother's will and that it deserves the same chance to live as a child whose parents planned to conceive it. Some pro-life supporters, including politicians such as Rick Santorum and Richard Mourdock, have stated that when a child is created as a result of rape, that pregnancy is something God intended to happen; they believe the child is a gift from God and should be accepted and loved by the woman who was raped. Pro-choice supporters argue that a child whose mother was a victim of rape and who may not be prepared to support them could suffer from psychological damage.

The Right to Decide

The basic pro-choice position centers on the belief that the life of the fetus should not be given more consideration than the rights of the mother. Pro-choice advocates believe a woman's reproductive rights include access to sex education; the right to choose a safe, legal abortion; access to contraceptives; and the power to control her own body. They do not believe the government should be able to interfere with a woman's decision to have an abortion at all.

Difficulty Understanding

Some lawmakers have shown a lack of understanding about pregnancy and abortion, which has caused them to propose laws that many pro-choice advocates believe are unfair. In 2012, former Missouri Congressman Todd Akin said he did not feel abortion should be legal for victims of rape because he believed rape generally does not result in pregnancy. He said, "If it's legitimate rape, the female body has ways to try to shut the whole thing down."[1] This statement caused much controversy, even among other pro-life advocates, for several reasons. First, it implied that if a woman who said she was raped had a child, then the rape was not real. This put false blame on the rape victim. Second, medical professionals confirmed that his statement was untrue; it is entirely possible for a pregnancy to result from rape.

Todd Akin, shown here, has made remarks that show a lack of understanding of the relationship between rape and pregnancy.

In one study conducted in 1996, researchers found that rape-related pregnancy "occurs with significant frequency … It is a cause of many unwanted pregnancies and is closely linked with family and domestic violence."[2] The study found that about 5 percent of rape victims between the ages of 12 and 45–the ages at which most women can conceive a child–resulted in pregnancy. Although the percentage may seem small, it represents about 32,000 pregnancies per year.

1. Quoted in Lori Moore, "Rep. Todd Akin: The Statement and the Reaction," *New York Times*, August 20, 2012. www.nytimes.com/2012/08/21/us/politics/rep-todd-akin-legitimate-rape-statement-and-reaction.htm.

2. Quoted in Susan Perry, "Rape, Pregnancy Statistics and the Ignorance of Some Politicians," *MinnPost*, June 13, 2013. www.minnpost.com/second-opinion/2013/06/rape-pregnancy-statistics-and-ignorance-some-politicians.

Those with a pro-choice viewpoint see abortion as a private medical decision that should be made by a woman and her doctor without government interference. Sometimes pro-life supporters refer to pro-choice supporters as being pro-abortion, but this is a misleading term. Being pro-abortion would mean believing pregnant women should be encouraged or required to get an abortion, but few, if any, people feel this way. In 1992, when Bill Clinton ran for president, his vice presidential candidate Al Gore said, "Bill Clinton and I support the right of a woman to choose … That doesn't mean we're pro-abortion; in fact, we believe there are way too many abortions in this country."[2] Many pro-choice advocates believe abortion should be available to women who need it, but they hope increased use of contraceptives and sex education will decrease the rate of unplanned pregnancies, which will in turn decrease the rate of abortions. Other pro-choice supporters support the use of birth control, but believe it is a separate issue. People with this belief generally feel that abortion is a normal, common medical procedure and should simply be normalized rather than seen as a shameful or immoral thing.

In her 1999 remarks to NARAL Pro-Choice America, Clinton's wife and fellow politician Hillary Clinton voiced the pro-choice viewpoint by saying, "Being pro-choice is trusting the individual to make the right decision for herself and her family, and not entrusting that decision to anyone wearing the authority of government in any regard."[3] During her campaign for president in 2016, Hillary reaffirmed her commitment to provide abortion access to women. She said, "I will defend *Roe v. Wade* … and I will defend women's rights to make their own healthcare decisions."[4]

Pro-choice advocates believe there are many factors that go into a woman's choice about whether or not to have an abortion, and morality is only one of them. They believe, for example, a woman who does not want to raise a child or who feels unable to raise a child given her personal circumstances should have access to a safe, legal abortion if she chooses. Raising a child is something that will change a woman's life, and in order to provide a good life for her child, she must have enough time, money, and support from loved ones. A woman who is living in poverty and barely able to support herself will have a hard time providing her child with everything they need, and this will cause a lot of stress for the mother. Additionally, if a woman does not want a child, she may feel resentful instead of loving. Pro-choice supporters argue that the availability of safe, legal abortions ultimately reduces the number of children in foster care due to abuse and neglect.

Many pro-choice organizations choose to focus their attention on reducing the number of unintended pregnancies through comprehensive sex education in high schools, the use of contraceptives, and greater parental involvement. In their view, limited sex education programs without instruction in the use of contraceptives actually increases the demand for abortions rather than decreasing it: The fewer people who know how to use contraceptives, the more unintended pregnancies there will be, and therefore, the more abortions there will be. George Monbiot wrote in *The Guardian*, "The most effective means of preventing the deaths of unborn children is to promote contraception."[5]

Many pro-choice supporters also support teaching young adults about contraception.

Pro-choice supporters often express frustration with pro-life groups because they believe they ignore many of the social ills created when parents are unwilling or unable to care for their unintended children adequately. Some people who oppose abortion also oppose welfare—financial assistance or free goods and services the government gives people who live in poverty—as well as contraception. Welfare refers to a specific program called Temporary Assistance for Needy Families (TANF), but the term is often misused to refer to all government assistance, including SNAP (commonly referred to as food stamps) and Medicaid. For this reason, pro-choice supporters often say many pro-life supporters only care about the fetus, not the child it develops into. In 2017, *Slate* published a criticism of the pro-life movement's focus on Christian values, despite the fact that not everyone shares those values. The author quoted a Catholic nun named Sister Joan Chittister:

> *I do not believe that just because you're opposed to abortion, that that makes you pro-life. In fact, I think in many cases, your morality is deeply lacking if all you want is a child born but not a child fed, not a child educated, not a child housed. And why would I think that you don't? Because you don't want any tax money to go there. That's not pro-life. That's pro-birth. We need a much broader conversation on what the morality of pro-life is.*[6]

These words are true of some pro-life supporters, but not all. However, news shows often feature people who hold this view, so it is the view people most often associate with the pro-life movement. News shows tend to feature people who hold the most controversial opinions on any position because it attracts more viewers, which increases the news network's profits. In reality, pro-life supporters hold a wide variety of opinions about the different issues involved in the abortion discussion. For instance, Catholics are a group commonly associated with the pro-life movement, and Catholic teaching states that couples should not use birth control. However, a Gallup poll conducted in 2012 found that 82 percent of Catholics believe birth control is morally acceptable, and many Catholic women use it.

Life versus Personhood

Although some people talk a lot about when life begins, others argue that the real question is not when life begins, but when the fetus becomes a person. Scientists do not necessarily agree on when this happens. According to *Wired* magazine, "An embryologist might say gastrulation, which is when an embryo can no longer divide to form identical twins. A neuroscientist might say when one can measure brainwaves. As a doctor, [Diane] Horvath-Cosper says, 'I have come to the conclusion that the pregnant woman gets to decide when it's a person.'"[7] Many pro-choice individuals believe the mother's reproductive rights and the right to control her own body override any rights of the fetus. Some pro-life advocates may feel life begins at conception, but they may also believe that a zygote is not a person yet and therefore is not the same as a newborn.

Many pro-choice advocates believe a woman should be able to have an abortion at any point in her pregnancy, although some feel abortion should be illegal after 24 weeks, which is when a baby would generally be able to survive outside the womb on its own. Late-term abortions—those done after this time limit has passed—have been especially controversial, and many states have banned them.

"The Only Moral Abortion Is My Abortion"

It is not unheard of for pro-life supporters to get an abortion if they get pregnant and feel that in their situation, an abortion would not be immoral. Joyce Arthur, the founder and executive director of the Abortion Rights Coalition of Canada, wrote an article titled "The Only Moral Abortion Is My Abortion," which included stories from abortion clinic workers about this topic. One story came from a clinic escort in Massachusetts:

> In 1990, in the Boston area, Operation Rescue and other groups were regularly blockading the clinics,

and many of us went every Saturday morning for months to help women and staff get in. As a result, we knew many of the "antis" by face. One morning, a woman who had been a regular "sidewalk counselor" went into the clinic with a young woman who looked like she was 16-17, and obviously her daughter. When the mother came out about an hour later, I had to go up and ask her if her daughter's situation had caused her to change her mind. "I don't expect you to understand my daughter's situation!" she angrily replied. The following Saturday, she was back, pleading with women entering the clinic not to "murder their babies."[1]

Another story came from a doctor in the Netherlands: "I once had a German client who greatly thanked me at the door, leaving after a difficult 22-week abortion. With a gleaming smile, she added: 'Und doch sind Sie ein Mörderer.' ('And you're still a murderer.')"[2] These stories show that personal experiences and professed beliefs do not always match up. There are many reasons why someone may get an abortion despite stating that they are pro-life. Some may feel guilty afterward and see their own abortion as something morally wrong; others may believe their specific situation is unique and therefore not morally wrong. In fact, in 1981—the last time a study was done on this topic—the results "found that 24% of women who had abortions considered the procedure morally wrong, and 7% of women who'd had abortions disagreed with the statement, 'Any woman who wants an abortion should be permitted to obtain it legally.'"[3]

1. Quoted in Joyce Arthur, "The Only Moral Abortion Is My Abortion: When the Anti-Choice Chooses," Pro Choice Action Network, September 2000, www.prochoiceactionnetwork-canada.org/articles/anti-tales.shtml.
2. Quoted in Arthur, "The Only Moral Abortion Is My Abortion."
3. Arthur, "The Only Moral Abortion Is My Abortion."

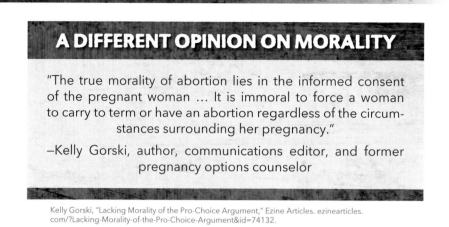

A DIFFERENT OPINION ON MORALITY

"The true morality of abortion lies in the informed consent of the pregnant woman ... It is immoral to force a woman to carry to term or have an abortion regardless of the circumstances surrounding her pregnancy."

–Kelly Gorski, author, communications editor, and former pregnancy options counselor

Kelly Gorski, "Lacking Morality of the Pro-Choice Argument," Ezine Articles. ezinearticles. com/?Lacking-Morality-of-the-Pro-Choice-Argument&id=74132.

Public Views versus Private Views

Because there are so many opinions about when life begins and at what point it must morally be preserved, it is unlikely there will be agreement any time soon. Political parties, politicians, and abortion interest groups will continue their debate. Every day, decisions will continue to be made about abortion on a personal level. These decisions are intensely private. What a person may say in public about abortion may differ from how they view it for themselves.

For a number of years now, polls have consistently shown most Americans have no desire to overturn the *Roe v. Wade* decision of 1973. Americans, in general, appear to believe abortion should remain legal and be left to the discretion of a woman and her doctor throughout some or all of the gestation period. When a 2017 Pew Research Center poll asked Americans if they supported the Supreme Court's *Roe v. Wade* decision, 69 percent answered yes.

A different answer, however, is often given when pollsters ask a slightly different question. When asked if they believe abortion to be right or wrong, 44 percent of those surveyed said they thought it was wrong. Another 19 percent believed it was morally acceptable, and 34 percent said it was not a moral issue at all. This is a surprising revelation, considering most Americans believe abortion, at least in some cases, should be legal. Some Americans appear to believe abortion is wrong on a personal level but believe others should be free to make whatever choice fits their own situation.

Abortion is considered by many to be a private decision. People who believe this tend to feel that the government should not make this decision for a woman.

The morality question is apparently one the majority of Americans consider to be a private decision. They are reluctant for government to have any part of it. With the loss of what they view as a personal freedom at the hands of their government, they fear losing other personal freedoms would be inevitable.

Timothy Johnson is a medical contributor for ABC News who appeared regularly on the ABC network to explain medical and health issues. He has found that he, like so many other Americans, is of two minds when it comes to the issue of abortion. He said, "I find myself saying that I am anti-abortion but also pro-choice. I do find the idea and act of abortion distasteful or even offensive. And I recognize that it destroys a life in the making. But … I support the right of each woman to decide what is the right choice for her."[8]

What About Adoption?

Adoption is seen by many people on both sides of the debate to be morally acceptable. According to the March for Life, a group who takes part in an annual political march to protest the legalization of abortion, "when a mother chooses adoption over abortion, birthmom, adoptive parents, and the baby all benefit tremendously from her decision."[1] Many pro-choice advocates also believe part of the freedom to choose means a woman should be allowed to make the choice to place her baby for adoption.

However, the two sides often disagree on certain things about adoption. For instance, many pro-life advocates believe adoption is a moral alternative to abortion and may try to convince a woman that giving birth and placing the baby for adoption is a better decision than abortion. However, many pro-choice advocates believe a woman should not be forced to give birth if she does not want to, even if she does not have to raise the child herself afterward. Pregnancy still affects a woman's life and body; for example, a woman may get so nauseous during her pregnancy that she is not able to go to work or school. Additionally, some people feel the adoption process is unfair; for instance, if an adoptive couple finds they are not yet ready to take care of the child they have adopted, they may place the child into foster care, which may result in the child having a difficult life.

1. "Adoption," March for Life, accessed July 20, 2017. marchforlife.org/adoption-a-noble-decision/.

Clearly, the abortion debate rages not only on a national and political level, but on a very personal one as well. Journalist Anna Quindlen summed it up by saying, "And that is where I find myself now, in the middle—hating the idea of abortion, hating the idea of having them outlawed."[9] Many people recognize her dilemma and share her frustration.

More than 40 years after the legalization of abortion, Americans are still struggling with both their private feelings and the legal aspects of this topic. Is abortion moral? On a personal level, the decision is a very private one, influenced by religious beliefs, marital or economic status, available resources, health, and many other considerations. Publicly, however, the morality of abortion is likely to continue to be a point of debate for years to come.

The Debate over Government Involvement

Although people debate whether or not someone should get an abortion, a separate debate is whether or not the government should be involved in that decision. Many pro-choice advocates believe abortion should be legal and that the government should help women, especially low-income women, get one if they need one. This kind of help can involve requiring health insurance companies to cover an abortion so it is less expensive; it can also involve not restricting access to abortion facilities. Many pro-choice advocates also believe the government should require employers and health insurance companies to cover birth control so women can avoid the question of an abortion altogether.

Pro-life advocates, in contrast, generally believe the government should do everything possible to prevent people from getting an abortion, including making it a crime. Some pro-life supporters also believe an employer should not be required to provide birth control, especially if the company is religious. There are many debates about the consequences of all of these decisions.

A Dangerous Time

At the time of U.S. independence, the only laws on abortion were those of common law (adopted from England and based on legal decisions of the past). Common law favored the idea of abortion being acceptable as long as it occurred before the first time the mother felt the baby move—an event that was known as quickening. James Wilson, one of the authors of the Constitution, a lawyer, and one of the original justices on the

Some people believe it is the government's job to weigh in on the abortion debate, while others believe the government has no business getting involved in the issue.

Supreme Court, expressed the views of the Founding Fathers in a paper entitled *Of the Natural Rights of Individuals.* In it, he wrote, "In the contemplation of law, life begins when the infant is first able to stir in the womb. By the law, life is protected … from every degree of danger."[10]

By the 1820s, anti-abortion laws began to appear in various states. During this time, Connecticut passed a law aimed at stopping the sale of poisons to women for abortion purposes. A few years later, New York made post-quickening abortions a felony. In the late 1800s, the trend toward making abortion illegal continued to gain momentum, and by 1900, abortion at any stage of pregnancy was illegal in most states, although some did allow the practice under limited circumstances. Some laws also made birth control illegal as well as information regarding sex education, family planning, and abortion. At the time, anything having to do with sex was considered obscene, or disgusting, so an 1873 law called the Comstock Act banned such information from being published. As a result, many people were not well informed about how to prevent pregnancy.

The fact that abortions were illegal, however, did not stop them from occurring. At the time, an unmarried woman who had a child suffered much criticism and social isolation, since people believed women who had sex outside of marriage were immoral. Illegal abortions—which are sometimes referred to as "back-alley" abortions, although they generally did not actually take place in alleys—continued to be available for those who had the means to afford them. The Guttmacher Institute estimates 200,000 to 1.2 million illegal abortions a year were performed from 1950 to 1970. These procedures were often unsafe and sometimes resulted in disability, infertility, or even death. In 1965, about 200 women died from complications of illegal abortions. Even those who did not die sometimes experienced negative side effects and judgment from others. Still, this did not stop them from seeking out illegal abortion clinics, as they believed the side effects were better than the prospect of giving birth and raising a child. A 61-year-old woman named Susan recalled the illegal abortion she had in 1970, when she was 19 years old. After she was raped, Susan did not want to have her rapist's baby, especially since she did not have a support system of family and friends. She said,

> My life stopped entirely. I just stayed at home curled up in a chair, too fearful to sleep during the night and too ashamed to connect with any of my friends … Finally, I received an appointment at the local hospital. I went alone … another horrible, isolating experience. The whispers, stares and insensitivity of the nursing staff was devastating … I bled heavily for a month afterwards, I passed large pieces of tissue and was very scared. One night I passed out, I believe, from the loss of blood. The doctor who performed the abortion refused me a follow-up appointment. I was too ashamed to go to another doctor for help. Somehow I survived … Do I have any regrets? No. Am I sorry? Absolutely not! That abortion allowed me a second chance … to get on with my life.[11]

Women who could not afford to have a doctor perform an abortion or did not know where to find someone who would perform the procedure illegally sometimes tried dangerous methods of doing it themselves. These included drinking toxic chemicals and inserting a sharp object into the uterus, which had the possibility of puncturing the uterine wall and causing dangerous internal bleeding. This is why self-induced abortions are often called "coat hanger abortions," as a coat hanger was a sharp object most women had readily available. The fear of unsafe abortion procedures led some groups to provide secret abortion services.

One of the best-known examples was a group of women in Chicago who operated a secret abortion clinic between 1969 and 1973. Officially called the Abortion Counseling Service of Women's Liberation but nicknamed the Jane Collective, the clinic originally made arrangements for women to have the procedure done in secret by doctors who performed abortions. One of the founders told Laura Kaplan, the author of *The Story of Jane*, that she decided to help start the group because there were no women involved in the process and she felt the men could not understand the point of view of a woman who wanted an abortion. Over time, the creators of the group learned to perform abortions themselves because at the time, many of the men who called themselves doctors had not actually earned that title and did not know how to perform abortions safely; they did it because the job paid well. At the height of the group's success, the women were performing as many as 60 abortions per week, risking arrest every time they performed the procedure since it was still illegal at the time.

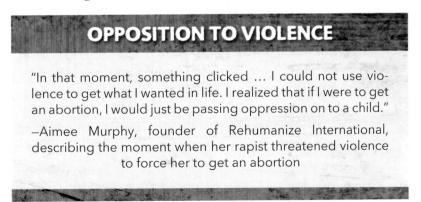

OPPOSITION TO VIOLENCE

"In that moment, something clicked ... I could not use violence to get what I wanted in life. I realized that if I were to get an abortion, I would just be passing oppression on to a child."

—Aimee Murphy, founder of Rehumanize International, describing the moment when her rapist threatened violence to force her to get an abortion

Quoted in Ruth Graham, "The New Culture of Life," *Slate*, October 11, 2016. www.slate.com/articles/double_x/cover_story/2016/10/the_future_of_the_pro_life_movement.html.

The Impact of *Roe v. Wade*

By the beginning of the 1970s, some states were beginning to legalize abortion for situations involving rape or incest and for cases in which the woman's life or health were endangered by her pregnancy. Other states adopted less restrictive laws allowing abortions for reasons other than for these extreme cases. This caused significant differences in abortion regulations from state to state.

In 1969, a 22-year-old Texas woman named Norma McCorvey was devastated to learn Texas was one of the states in which abortions were still illegal except in cases where the mother's life was in danger. Pregnant with her third child, McCorvey desperately tried to find an abortion provider but was unsuccessful. Instead, she became the plaintiff in a landmark lawsuit challenging the Texas law prohibiting abortion and took on the pseudonym "Jane Roe" to protect her identity. At the time, McCorvey did not realize any victory in the case would come too late to allow her to have an abortion. Long before the case reached the Supreme Court, McCorvey's child had been born and given up for adoption.

A QUESTION OF RESPECT

"None of the [abortion] protestors asked me about my decision—and nothing they said that day made me not want to go through with it … They claimed to care about human beings, but they left no space for understanding or compassion. I believe that everyone has the right to share his or her views. I also think it can be done in a respectful and empathetic way."

—Ronak, abortion recipient

Quoted in Liz Welch, "6 Women on Their Terrifying, Infuriating Encounters with Abortion Clinic Protestors," *Cosmopolitan*, February 21, 2014. www.cosmopolitan.com/politics/news/a5669/abortion-clinic-protesters/.

In 1973, the U.S. Supreme Court ruled on the case that came to be known as *Roe v. Wade*. In its ruling, the Court stated that women, upon the advice of their doctors, had a constitutional right to have an abortion in the early stages of pregnancy. A pregnancy is divided into three trimesters of three months each. The first is weeks 0 to 12, the second is weeks 13 to 27, and the third is weeks 28 until the baby is born. The justices stated that a first trimester embryo was not a person under the Constitution and a woman's right to privacy included the right to an abortion. They further determined the states could intervene in second trimester abortions and outlaw them altogether in the third except in cases where the woman's life or health was at risk.

In a separate decision regarding *Roe v. Wade*'s companion case, *Doe v. Bolton*, the Court ruled threats to a woman's health could be physical, emotional, psychological, or familial (family related). This broad definition allowed any licensed doctor

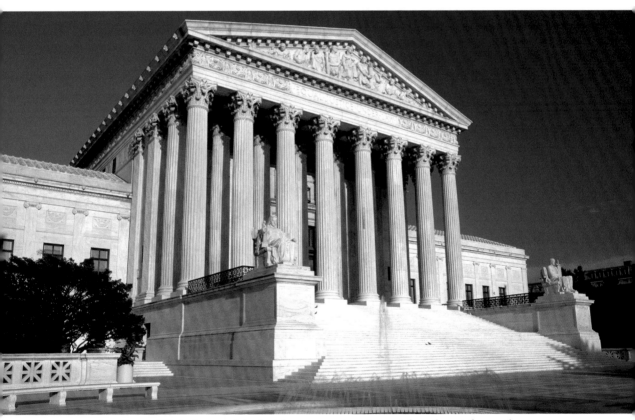

Roe v. Wade is one of the best known, most controversial, and most frequently discussed Supreme Court cases in history.

willing to perform an abortion the legal option to do so. In the wake of the Supreme Court's decision, the number of legal abortions rose sharply and continued to a peak of about 29.3 abortions per 1,000 women between 1980 and 1981. From that point on, the number began to decline slowly. By 2014, the number had fallen to 14.6 per 1,000 women—the lowest since *Roe v. Wade* was passed. Many pro-choice advocates believe this is due to increased access to contraception, while many pro-life supporters feel it is because some states have put restrictions on abortion.

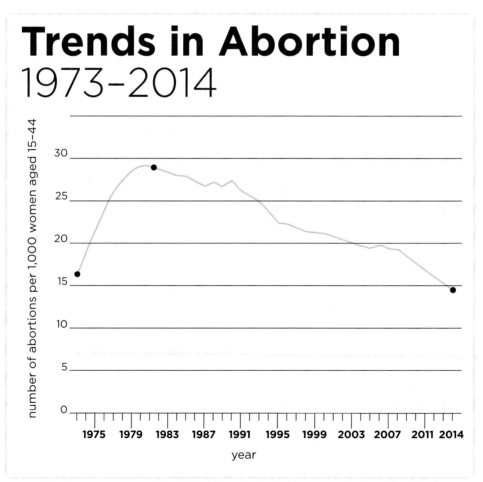

Trends in Abortion
1973-2014

The abortion rate in the United States has reached a historic low, as this information from the Guttmacher Institute shows.

Restrictions to Abortion Access

The Supreme Court did not revisit the issue of abortion again until 1992, when it heard the case of *Planned Parenthood of Southeastern Pennsylvania v. Casey*, which debated the right of states to make it harder for women to get an abortion. The decision in this case upheld a woman's right to an abortion as part of her liberty and privacy protected by the 14th Amendment. However, it also upheld many of the state's restrictions, such as requiring girls under 18 to get permission from at least one parent and a 24-hour waiting period. Since then, many other states have created restrictions that make it harder for women to get an abortion. Many pro-life advocates argue that there is nothing wrong with these restrictions because the states are upholding *Roe v. Wade*, not making abortion illegal. However, many pro-choice supporters fight the restrictions because they say it does not matter whether abortion is still legal if other laws effectively stop women from getting one. *Planned Parenthood of Southeastern Pennsylvania v. Casey* said restrictions could not cause an "undue burden" on a woman, which means restrictions cannot be put in place simply to block abortion access. However, as *The New Yorker* pointed out, "the standard has been applied weakly and inconsistently."[12]

The laws states have passed to restrict access apply only to abortions, not any other kind of medical procedure, so the laws are generally called Targeted Regulation of Abortion Providers (TRAP) laws. According to the Guttmacher Institute, a nonprofit organization that researches sexual and reproductive health worldwide, some of the restrictions various states have put in place include:

- requiring abortions to be performed by a licensed doctor

- requiring abortions to be performed in a hospital after a certain point in the pregnancy

- requiring a second doctor to help after a certain point in the pregnancy

- preventing private insurance plans from covering abortion for any reason other than endangerment of the life of the mother

- requiring women to go to counseling before getting an abortion

- waiting periods of at least 24 hours between receiving counseling and getting an abortion

- requiring clinics to meet the same standards as a hospital

Some people approve of laws such as these because they want it to be difficult for a woman to get an abortion or because they feel the laws benefit women; for instance, a pro-life person may feel that requiring an abortion to be performed by a doctor or in a hospital would make the procedure safer for the woman. Others feel these types of laws violate the undue burden portion of *Planned Parenthood of Southeastern Pennsylvania v. Casey* and should not be allowed. Restricting insurance coverage or requiring a hospital stay means a woman may not be able to afford an abortion, and requiring one or two doctors to perform the procedure means a clinic that does not have enough doctors on staff may not be able to offer abortions, even though a nurse practitioner would also have the knowledge to perform them safely. In the case of medical abortions (as opposed to surgical abortions), the process involves simply taking a pill, which means that going to a hospital or requiring a doctor to prescribe it—when a nurse practitioner or physician's assistant is licensed to do so—is unnecessary.

Elizabeth Nash, state issues manager at the Guttmacher Institute, said, "These restrictions have an uneven impact ... Women who have resources, have a car, have some money in the bank ... and take time off work can obtain an abortion, and women who are less well-off and don't have those kinds of resources are not able to access abortion services."[13] Nash and other pro-choice advocates believe some of the state requirements should be removed to make abortion access easier,

Dilation and Extraction

Beginning in 1995, the U.S. Congress made several attempts to pass federal laws banning a particular type of abortion—intact dilation and extraction, sometimes abbreviated to D&X. Also known as partial-birth abortion, this procedure involves removing the fetus from the woman's birth canal before the fetus is viable (able to live on its own outside the womb). In 2007, the Supreme Court upheld a nationwide ban, ruling it did not conflict with previous Court decisions. Some states have also enforced extra harsh penalties for D&X abortions. Dilation and extraction is not the same as dilation and evacuation (D&E), which is the most common type of abortion performed in the second trimester. Most pro-choice and pro-life advocates agree that D&X abortions are not desirable.

In a 2016 debate between presidential candidates Donald Trump and Hillary Clinton, the candidates were asked whether they supported "late-term, partial-birth abortions."[1] *Forbes* magazine explained some of the problems with this question:

> *"Partial birth" is a political, not medical, term, and it does not refer to all late-term abortions. It refers to a very specific and rare procedure called dilation and extraction … nearly always when the fetus cannot live outside the womb and typically when the mother's health is in danger, the fetus has a serious abnormality, or both. Such a procedure is not conducted lightly: the fetus has a fatal defect and will not survive, or the mother is at risk of death herself.[2]*

1. Quoted in Tara Haelle, "No, Late-Term Abortions Don't 'Rip' Babies Out of Wombs—and They Exist for a Reason," *Forbes*, October 20, 2016. www.forbes.com/sites/tarahaelle/2016/10/20/no-late-term-abortions-dont-rip-babies-out-of-wombs-but-they-are-needed/#3b0b80525cf8

2. Haelle, "No, Late-Term Abortions Don't 'Rip' Babies Out of Wombs."

pointing out that it does not matter if abortion is legal if someone is unable to get to a place that performs the procedure. In some states, laws requiring clinics to renovate to meet the same standards as a hospital—for instance, widening doorways to make room for wheelchairs, even if no wheelchairs are used at the clinic—have caused many abortion clinics to shut down because the renovations are generally too expensive for them to perform. In states such as Texas, where the remaining abortion clinics are spread far apart, a woman may have to drive more than five hours to get to one. If there is a waiting period, she will either have to drive home and then come back another day or get a hotel room and wait. For someone with no car and little money, neither of these may be a possibility. Additionally, one study of patients who had to wait 72 hours in Utah found that the waiting period caused increased distress and financial burden for women:

> Because of appointment availability and the logistical challenges inherent in going to a clinic and returning exactly three days later, the waiting period caused an average of eight days of waiting; this led to increased anxiety for patients, who were then pushed further into their pregnancies. And because the price of an abortion increases weekly, waiting that extra time pushed the costs for the procedure 10 percent higher than they would have been had patients been able to access the service sooner.[14]

An abortion can be difficult for people to afford in the United States and in many places around the world.

Many pro-life advocates blame the abortion clinics for their own closures. Kristi Hamrick, a spokesperson for Americans United for Life (AUL), said, "It was the choice of the abortion industry to locate their profitable abortion businesses in older buildings that would never pass muster for other outpatient surgical procedures."[15] Hamrick and other pro-life advocates say they would rather have fewer, safer abortion clinics than more clinics that may not be as safe. Pro-choice advocates argue that the renovations are unnecessary, are designed to force clinics to close to prevent women from accessing abortions, and do not have any effect on the safety of the procedure. In fact, many argue, restricting access will simply force many women to resort to unsafe self-induced abortions of the kind *Roe v. Wade* was intended to prevent. This debate will likely continue for the foreseeable future.

The Pro-Life Opinion

Pro-life advocates do not believe abortion is a right guaranteed by the Constitution. Instead, they point out that because the Constitution is silent on the subject, the current basis for abortion rights is an implied right subject to the interpretation of the Court. In a widely read 1984 essay titled *Abortion and the Conscience of the Nation*, President Ronald Reagan voiced the pro-life viewpoint by saying, "Make no mistake, abortion-on-demand is not a right granted by the Constitution. No serious scholar, including one disposed to agree with the Court's result, has argued that the framers of the Constitution intended to create such a right."[16]

Pro-life supporters believe a woman's right to privacy and control of her own body stops at the point where it affects a life other than her own. In their view, the developing fetus is another person completely separate from the mother, dependent on her only for food and shelter—just as if it were already born. They believe the rights of all individuals must be considered, including those of persons who are not yet born.

Some pro-life advocates are convinced abortion devalues human life prior to birth and could lead to the devaluation of human life at other stages. If a human fetus has no rights, they argue, who will be next? Will some future society determine other members of society to be of no value and therefore unnecessary? By not placing restrictions on abortion, some pro-life advocates believe a dangerous precedent is being established that might one day lead to the destruction of handicapped individuals, the elderly, the homeless, or some other segment of society labeled as unwanted or unnecessary. Other pro-life advocates, especially people whose views are shaped by their religion, view all life as sacred and in need of protection. These people see abortion as being equal to murder.

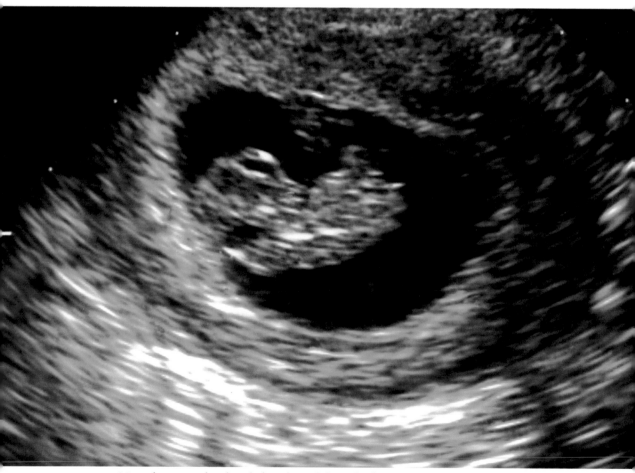

Most abortions take place before the eighth week of pregnancy. This ultrasound shows what the fetus looks like at almost nine weeks.

Pro-life advocates believe *Roe v. Wade* and *Doe v. Bolton* should be overturned. They cite the language of the Constitution itself, and the 14th Amendment in particular, as the basis for protecting the life of the unborn. They believe the framers of the Constitution had the unborn in mind when they declared their intent to "secure the blessings of liberty to ourselves and our posterity" in the preamble. They believe these words identify the unborn as worthy of the same right to "life, liberty, and the pursuit of happiness" as any other American.

ARE WAITING PERIODS UNNECESSARY?

"If a patient says they need more time, we're happy to give them time ... But a state mandating that everyone who comes in needs more time is insulting to women, it's demeaning, it makes the process a lot more complex, and it's medically unnecessary."

–Dr. Bhavik Kumar, physician at Whole Women's Health in Texas

Quoted in Gina Pollack, "What It's Like to Endure a Forced Waiting Period Before Your Abortion," *Broadly*, April 26, 2016. broadly.vice.com/en_us/article/qkg753/what-its-like-to-endure-a-forced-waiting-period-before-your-abortion.

The Pro-Choice Opinion

Those with a pro-choice viewpoint tend to see the question of constitutional rights from a completely different angle. They believe a woman's right to privacy and reproductive control are protected by the 14th Amendment. On the basis of this amendment, the 1965 case of *Griswold v. Connecticut* determined that liberty included the concept of personal privacy. Pro-choice supporters believe this includes a woman's right to make her own reproductive decisions, including whether to carry her pregnancy to term or to have an abortion. In their view, any limitations placed on abortion access are a clear violation of constitutional rights.

Aside from the question of rights, many pro-choice advocates also have a fear of having the religious or philosophical beliefs of a single group forced on everyone. While many pro-choice individuals acknowledge abortion is not the best option for everyone, they believe the decision is a private one to be made by a woman with the advice of her doctor or other medical adviser. It is not, they argue, a decision that should be subject to public opinion or debate.

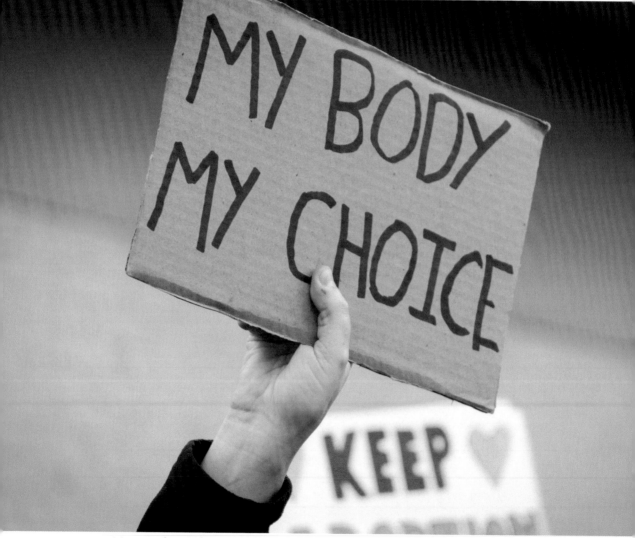

Most pro-choice advocates believe anti-abortion laws infringe on a woman's right to make her own medical decisions.

As far as pro-choice supporters are concerned, *Roe v. Wade* should stand as is. They believe the legal restrictions of the last decade have rendered the 1973 decision less effective. Pro-choice advocates strongly believe in the Supreme Court's original decision—that a woman's right to privacy extends to her decision to terminate a pregnancy if she chooses to do so. Overturning *Roe v. Wade* to make abortion illegal once again would serve no constructive purpose, they argue, since studies have shown making it illegal does not have any impact on the number of abortions actually performed. "Evidence from around the world shows that placing restrictions on abortion to make it harder to obtain has much more to do with making it less safe than making it rarer,"[17] said Susan Cohen, former vice president for public policy at the Guttmacher Institute.

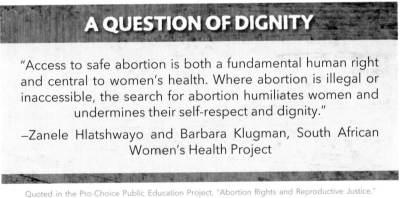

A QUESTION OF DIGNITY

"Access to safe abortion is both a fundamental human right and central to women's health. Where abortion is illegal or inaccessible, the search for abortion humiliates women and undermines their self-respect and dignity."

–Zanele Hlatshwayo and Barbara Klugman, South African Women's Health Project

Quoted in the Pro-Choice Public Education Project, "Abortion Rights and Reproductive Justice." www.protectchoice.org/article.php?id=130.

Illegal abortions, pro-choice supporters point out, are still abortions. Making them illegal would only result in "underground" services such as the ones prior to 1973. This, they fear, would likely be unsafe and allow opportunists to take advantage of women at a time when they are most vulnerable. They believe a ban on abortions would ultimately cause much harm to women's individual health and their health care in general.

Ethical Dilemmas

There are many separate issues involved in the abortion debate and many different sides to each issue. People may hold a variety of views on these issues. For instance, two pro-life people who agree that mandatory counseling before an abortion is a good thing may disagree on whether insurance companies should cover birth control pills. The issues surrounding abortion are extremely controversial and often lead to fights between people who hold opposite opinions. An agreement may never be reached, but understanding another person's point of view is still important.

NORMALIZING MALE BIRTH CONTROL

"What if it became common practice for 16-year-old boys to talk to their fathers about getting 'that prescription,' just as many girls do with their mothers? Maybe young men might even start viewing sex in a more serious, responsible light."

—Alex Mar, author and filmmaker

Alex Mar, "Jagged Little Pill: Will Male Birth Control Ever Become a Reality?," Slate, October 1, 2004. slate.com/id/2107558.

Understanding Pregnancy

In the years before *Roe v. Wade*, Americans were generally un-educated about matters relating to sexuality and childbirth. Many of the topics discussed openly in today's society were considered unmentionable. Types of birth control were limited and not readily available, especially for the very poor or the very young, and the ones that were available were riskier than they are today; for instance, the hormone levels in birth control pills were higher, leading to increased side effects. This influenced many women to avoid many types of birth control completely.

Today, the general public is more informed about birth control, abortion, and fetal development. Due to scientific advancements, the number of birth control and abortion options has greatly increased, and they are safer and more effective. Americans expressing an opinion today are far more likely to have an informed opinion than they were 35 years ago. However, some myths still remain. Some of these myths are promoted by people who support one opinion or another and want to spread misinformation to sway other people to their cause, but other myths persist through a lack of education and some people's unwillingness to learn more about things they disapprove of.

Protests and Violence

Some pro-life supporters protest outside abortion clinics, shouting and holding anti-abortion signs so women going inside to get advice or an abortion can see them. They believe seeing these messages will make women think twice about their abortion. However, in many cases, these protests simply cause psychological distress to the women entering the clinic, even the ones who are not there to get an abortion. Some clinics have recruited volunteers to escort women into the clinic so they feel safer walking past the protestors. When a 27-year-old woman named Marie went to a Planned Parenthood in Maine to pick up her birth control pills, she saw protestors outside the clinic. Marie said, "As I started to walk towards the clinic, one woman followed me all the way to the door, saying, 'Have mercy on your baby ... ' My heart was racing—I was actually scared, but then I saw two women flanking the door, wearing pink vests. One smiled at me, and I kept my eyes locked on her until I finally made it inside."[1] In February 2017, when large anti-abortion rallies were held outside Planned Parenthood locations across the country, counter-protestors arrived as well to show their support for Planned Parenthood.

A few pro-life advocates have resorted to violence, bombing abortion clinics and shooting doctors who perform abortions. According to the *New York Times*, 11 people had been killed in abortion clinic attacks between 1993 and 2015. Eric Rudolph, a man who was sentenced to life in jail after he bombed an abortion clinic, said, "Abortion is murder ... And because it is murder I believe deadly force is needed to stop it."[2] Most people, including the majority of pro-life supporters, do not share this belief.

Many clinics ask volunteers to wait outside the doors so women who come in for appointments feel safer entering the building.

1. Quoted in Liz Welch, "6 Women on Their Terrifying, Infuriating Encounters with Abortion Clinic Protestors," *Cosmopolitan*, February 21, 2014. www.cosmopolitan.com/politics/news/a5669/ abortion-clinic-protesters/

2. Quoted in Michael E. Miller and Yanan Wang, "The Radical, Unrepentant Ideology of Abortion Clinic Killers," *Washington Post*, November 30, 2015. www.washingtonpost.com/news/morning-mix/ wp/2015/11/30/the-radical-unrepentant-ideology-of-abortion-clinic-killers/?utm_term=.780e8bcf5e24.

The Facts About Late-Term Abortion

Late-term abortions, which are performed after 24 weeks, or 20 weeks in some states, are a highly debated topic. They are generally performed when other types of abortions are no longer possible. Late-term procedures are much more invasive and present a greater risk to the pregnant woman, so most people agree it is better to avoid them.

About 92 percent of all abortions performed in the United States each year occur during the first trimester, since a woman generally decides almost immediately whether or not she wants to keep the baby. Second trimester abortions account for about 7 percent of the yearly total, and third trimester abortions make up only about 1 percent. In many second or third trimester—late-term—abortions, the woman either did not realize she was pregnant, needed time to save up the money for the procedure, was in an abusive relationship that she hoped would improve, or had some other reason for delaying. In many circumstances, medical tests revealed a potentially serious genetic defect in the fetus that would cause the baby to die soon after it was born, or the pregnancy was determined to threaten the health or life of the mother or the baby.

In a 2014 Gallup poll, 61 percent said first trimester abortions should be legal, 27 percent said second trimester abortions should be legal, and only 14 percent said third trimester abortions should be legal. Many pro-life supporters—and even some pro-choice supporters—oppose late-term abortions for a variety of reasons. Some people believe women want the option to get a late-term abortion because they are too lazy to get one earlier in their pregnancy, while others believe women want the option to change their minds about having a baby at any time. In 2016, presidential candidate Donald Trump showed a lack of understanding about what a late-term abortion means or how the procedure is done. In a presidential debate, he said, "If you go with what Hillary [Clinton] is saying, in the ninth month, you can take the baby and rip the baby out of the womb of the mother just prior to the birth of the baby."[18] In reality, Clinton did not support such a policy, and neither do pro-choice people.

Women generally only get late-term abortions when their life or the life of their child is in danger, and this type of abortion is typically a tragic event for the woman or couple, who hoped to be able to keep the baby.

Many people are unaware that the majority of late-term abortions are performed on women who wanted to give birth. When this happens within a relationship, it is an upsetting experience for both partners.

The website Jezebel published an interview with a woman named Elizabeth who had to get an abortion at 32 weeks. She was thrilled when she found out she was pregnant, and throughout her pregnancy, she had been seeing her doctor and regularly getting ultrasounds and other tests to monitor the baby's progress. The baby had several abnormalities, such as malformed feet, but Elizabeth and the doctors remained hopeful that those could be corrected after birth. However, at 31 weeks, the doctor told Elizabeth that the baby had stopped growing and, if the baby was born, would not be able to breathe. The baby would die outside her womb in a matter of minutes. She described making her decision to have a late-term abortion:

> I was already going to have a C-section no matter what, because two years ago, I'd had brain surgery. And my doctor checked with the neurosurgeon, who wouldn't sign off on a natural birth. They were afraid that if I pushed, something might go in my head, so the delivery had to be a C-section. And so we were considering putting me through major abdominal surgery for a baby that's not going to make it, or risking that I go into natural labor and something pops in my head and I die, basically.
>
> To be clear, if the doctors thought there was any way he might make it, I would have taken that chance. I truly would have put myself through anything. What I came to accept was the fact that I would never get to be this little guy's mother—that if we came to term, he would likely live a very short time until he choked and died, if he even made it that far. This was a no-go for me. I couldn't put him through that suffering when we had the option to minimize his pain as much as possible.[19]

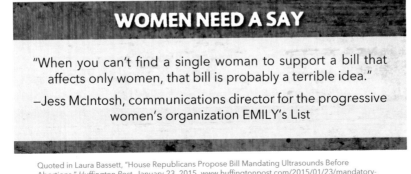

WOMEN NEED A SAY

"When you can't find a single woman to support a bill that affects only women, that bill is probably a terrible idea."

—Jess McIntosh, communications director for the progressive women's organization EMILY's List

Quoted in Laura Bassett, "House Republicans Propose Bill Mandating Ultrasounds Before Abortions," *Huffington Post*, January 23, 2015. www.huffingtonpost.com/2015/01/23/mandatory-ultrasound-_n_6535076.html.

When Women Have Abortions
in Weeks from Their Last Menstrual Period

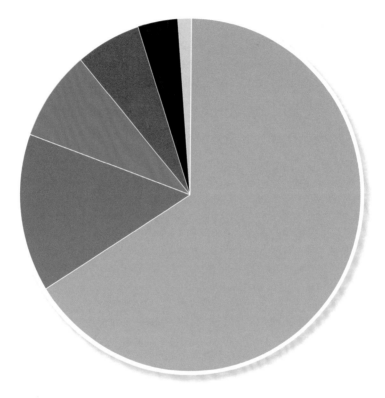

number of weeks	percentage
☐ ≤ 8	66%
☐ 9–10	14.5%
☐ 11–12	8.3%
☐ 13–15	6.2%
◼ 16–20	3.8%
☐ ≥ 21	1.3%

The majority of abortions take place before eight weeks, as this information from the Guttmacher Institute shows.

The Argument over Birth Control

Some pro-life advocates, including many people who are religious, believe birth control—including condoms and the contraceptive pill—is immoral. Some religions teach that birth control goes against God's will when he commanded Adam and Eve to "be fruitful and multiply" in the Bible. Others feel it is wrong because they believe birth control causes an unintentional abortion by killing a zygote. Medical professionals have stated that this is untrue; birth control prevents the egg from being fertilized at all, and many forms of birth control prevent a woman from releasing an egg in the first place, so there is nothing to be fertilized. Still others believe birth control is immoral because they feel sexual intercourse should only take place within a marriage, and they fear readily available birth control will encourage unmarried people to have sex.

In contrast, many pro-choice advocates believe there is nothing wrong with birth control. In fact, they feel it is an important way to reduce the abortion rate by reducing the number of unintended pregnancies. Many people support giving out condoms for free in schools to encourage teens to have safe sex. Advocates for Youth, an organization that aims to raise awareness among young adults about sexual health, reported that "a study of New York City's school condom availability program found a significant increase in condom use among sexually active students but no increase in sexual activity."[20] Young adults who take abstinence pledges are just as likely as other young adults to be sexually active and less likely to have safe sex, leading to higher rates of pregnancy and abortion.

Abortion rates dropped steeply between 2008 and 2011, and many pro-life advocates credited this to new laws that restricted abortion access or campaigns to convince women to choose not to get an abortion. However, according to the Guttmacher Institute, the true reason was increased access to birth control. The organization pointed out that, contrary to the arguments of pro-life supporters, abortion restrictions could not have caused the abortion decrease because the laws went into effect in 2011, so they would have had no effect on the years before that, when the majority of the decrease happened. Additionally, abortion rates decreased even in states that did not pass new restrictions. Further, the birth rate did not increase during this period, which shows that women were having fewer unintended pregnancies rather than choosing to carry an unintended pregnancy to term.

Today, women have many forms of contraception to choose from, including pills, condoms, and IUDs. Experts recommend using more than one method.

The Guttmacher Institute believes a large part of this trend can be credited to a health insurance law passed by President Barack Obama called the Affordable Care Act (ACA), sometimes nicknamed Obamacare. Health insurance is a confusing, complex topic, but in the simplest terms possible, the law gave more people the option to get health insurance and required companies to cover birth control. Since many women no longer had to pay a lot of money to get birth control, more women started using it more often. The Institute said,

> Thanks to the ACA, the proportion of U.S. women of reproductive age who are uninsured dropped by more than one-fifth between 2013 and 2014 ... The ACA has also spurred significant improvements in private insurance plans' contraceptive coverage ... saving U.S. women nearly half a billion dollars in out-of-pocket costs for contraception in 2013 alone. Collectively, this evidence illustrates that more women can now choose a birth control method on the basis of which works best for them—as opposed to which they can afford.[21]

Should Planned Parenthood Be Defunded?

The question of where Planned Parenthood gets the money it uses to provide services such as contraception and abortion has been a highly controversial subject in the abortion debate. Some of Planned Parenthood's services are provided by funds from the federal government, which has made many pro-life advocates angry. They say they do not want their tax dollars to give assistance to an organization that provides abortions, and some of them also do not want to support an organization that provides birth control. This has led many pro-life supporters to call for the government to defund Planned Parenthood. According to The Heritage Foundation, an organization that promotes conservative public policies, "Congress should end federal taxpayer funding to Planned Parenthood affiliates and redirect those funds to health centers that provide health care for women without entanglement in abortion."[22]

Birth Control for Men

Currently, many people see birth control as a woman's responsibility. Most contraception methods, such as birth control pills and intrauterine devices (IUDs), are only available for women, and some men do not want to wear condoms, which means the woman may receive the blame if she forgets to take her birth control pill—and according to the *American Journal of Obstetrics & Gynecology*, more than half of women do forget at least once. Additionally, birth control may cause issues for some women because of the hormones in the majority of currently available treatments, including weight gain, mood swings, decreased interest in sex, and, in rare cases, fatal blood clots. Some women may not be able to use it at all; even when they do, no form of birth control is currently 100 percent effective, so it is considered wise to use two forms—for instance, an IUD and a condom. To help solve some of these problems, several companies are investigating nonhormonal birth control for men, and the first clinical trials are expected to begin in 2018. Condoms are still an important way to stop the spread of sexually transmitted diseases (STDs), but for men and women who have been tested and know they do not have any, these new male birth control methods may help prevent unintended pregnancies without the negative side effects of hormonal birth control.

One option is called Vasalgel, which is a gel that would be injected into the vas deferens (the tube that sperm swim through) in the scrotum. The gel blocks the release of sperm, so there would be no way for an egg to be fertilized. Some men reject this method because they are worried about pain, but medical professionals say the injection site would be numbed first, so the man would not feel any pain during the procedure. It is much less invasive than permanent birth control surgery for women, such as a tubal ligation—often referred to as "having your tubes tied"—or a vasectomy for men. Vasalgel is also a reversible treatment, so a man who decides to have children in the future could do so. Other methods being investigated include several nonhormonal pills that prevent the sperm from effectively fertilizing an egg.

Some men dislike the idea of having to take any form of birth control, and the long-held idea that birth control is a woman's responsibility has made it hard for companies to get funding for male birth control research. However, polls in multiple countries have shown that the majority of men are excited to have the option to take more control of their reproductive options—so much so that many are donating their own money to the Male Contraception Initiative, which plans to crowdfund smaller research projects, then "use the success from the initial crowdfunding to target larger donors, so that bigger projects can be funded."[1]

Many men and women would welcome the opportunity to share the responsibility of using birth control.

1. Aaron Hamlin, "The Male Pill Is Coming—and It's Going to Change Everything," *Telegraph*, October 24, 2016. www.telegraph.co.uk/women/sex/the-male-pill-is-coming—and-its-going-to-change-everything/

The majority of funding for Planned Parenthood—60 percent—comes from Medicaid, which is a federal health insurance program for people who do not make enough money to pay for health insurance themselves. When a woman with Medicaid coverage goes to Planned Parenthood, the organization submits a claim to Medicaid, and the federal government covers the cost. The rest of the funding comes from a program called Title X Family Planning Program, which is the only federal grant program dedicated exclusively to helping low-income people access reproductive health care. This program is what allows organizations such as Planned Parenthood to provide health care on a sliding fee scale, where the patient pays for services at a discounted rate or receives them for free, depending on what they can afford.

A federal law states that Medicaid and Title X cannot cover abortions except in cases of rape, incest, or to save the life of the mother, so no taxpayer dollars are paying for them; women have to pay the cost out of pocket. This can be a barrier to allowing low-income women access to abortion, which is why some pro-choice people want abortions to be covered by Medicaid as well as private insurance. Federal funding only provides health exams, cancer screenings, birth control, sexually transmitted disease (STD) testing, and education about contraception. Removing that funding would only block low-income women from receiving those services; if Planned Parenthood clinics shut down due to lack of funding, wealthier women would have the option to see a more expensive doctor, but low-income women would not. Additionally, Planned Parenthood has reported that it is the only health care provider in more than 20 percent of the counties where it operates, which means if its clinics close, people may have to travel several hours to get to the next health care provider. Low-income patients may not be able to afford to do this, and other health care clinics may not have the resources to handle the extra number of patients. People who want the government to continue supporting Planned Parenthood have been organizing protests and showing their support online with the hashtag #IStandWithPP.

Many rallies have been organized across the United States so people can show their support for continued government funding for Planned Parenthood.

PARENTS AND PERMISSION

"If a parent has the right to stop his or her children from tattooing or piercing their own bodies, it seems ridiculous that they do not also have the right to review the child's decision to have a much more invasive operation performed."

–Sarah Hargrove, Vanderbilt University

Sarah Hargrove, "Abortion: Is Parental Consent Necessary?," *Orbis*, October 15, 2003. www.vanderbiltorbis.com/media/storage/paper983/news/2003/10/15/UndefinedSection/ Abortion.Is.Parental.Consent.Necessary-2471656.shtml.

Controversial Laws

Some laws or proposed laws are supported by pro-life advocates and fought by pro-choice advocates. One of these laws involves requiring girls under 18 to notify or get permission from one or both parents before getting an abortion. As of 2016, 38 states had such laws in place. However, a judge or doctor can excuse the teen from having to notify or ask her parents if they feel the teen is mature enough to make the decision or if they believe she will suffer negative physical or mental consequences from telling her parents. This is called a judicial bypass. Many pro-choice advocates believe parental notification laws violate a teen's right to privacy, while many pro-life advocates believe teens are not able to make such an important decision for themselves. Those who support parental-consent laws argue that minors are required to have parental approval for most medical procedures, including dental work, flu shots, or even the dispensing of an aspirin at school. They also point out that parents are legally responsible for minors and would have to pay any medical expenses due to complications from the abortion if any should arise. They also worry complications could go untreated or misdiagnosed if parents are unaware an abortion has taken place.

Another law many pro-choice advocates oppose was proposed in 2015 and would require women to receive an ultrasound and view it before being allowed to schedule an abortion. A similar law was proposed in 2012; this one required women to get a transvaginal ultrasound before being allowed to schedule an abortion. This type of ultrasound involves inserting part of the ultrasound equipment into the vagina, and women who wanted an abortion would not have been able to refuse the procedure, so many women compared it to rape and the bill was not passed.

A third bill banned abortions after 20 weeks and, although it did make an exception in the case of rape, required a woman to have reported the rape to the police in order to qualify. Since many women do not report their rape for fear of the social consequences, this would have barred many women who were raped from getting an abortion.

A bill proposed in Ohio in 2016 that was commonly nicknamed "the heartbeat bill" would have banned abortion after a fetal heartbeat could be detected, which in some cases, can be as early as six weeks. John Kasich, the governor of Ohio, vetoed the bill because it "conflicts with Supreme Court decisions upholding the right to abortion at least until the point at which the fetus is viable."[23] He did sign another bill that banned abortion after 20 weeks, but even that may be overturned, since "viability is generally interpreted to be around 24 weeks."[24] Many pro-choice supporters protested the heartbeat bill because at six weeks, a woman often has not yet realized she is pregnant.

Many of these bills are proposed by male lawmakers, which makes many pro-choice advocates, especially women, angry.

WOMEN HAVE OTHER OPTIONS

"Women's health care services are available without entanglement in abortion. There are about 1,200 federally qualified health centers (FQHC) across the country that operate … in medically underserved areas, providing family planning services, cancer screenings, and women's health exams."

–Sarah Torre, visiting fellow, Richard and Helen DeVos Center for Religion and Civil Society

Sarah Torre, "Congress Should End Federal Funding to Planned Parenthood and Redirect It Toward Other Health Care Options," The Heritage Foundation, September 22, 2015. www.heritage.org/health-care-reform/report/congress-should-end-federal-funding-planned-parenthood-and-redirect-it.

They say the men do not have a proper understanding of what it would be like to have to carry an unintended pregnancy to term and that it is easy for someone who is not personally affected to tell someone else what to do. Many pro-choice supporters believe men should not have a say in abortion legislation.

People have protested the fact that many of the committees that propose abortion laws are made up entirely of men.

The Debates Continue

The abortion debate is clearly not a matter of a simple yes or no; it is not even one single debate. There are many questions surrounding the issue that require individual study. Decisions about these individual questions often result in conflicting answers. Pro-life supporters sometimes find themselves taking pro-choice stands, while pro-choice individuals are sometimes surprised to find themselves in agreement with a pro-life view. The questions about abortion are complex and difficult to answer. Forming an opinion or making a decision requires making hard choices.

Health Effects

Like any medical procedure, abortion has potential side effects, both physical and mental. Some of these are minor, while others may be more severe. Some people experience no side effects at all; others do not suffer from the procedure itself, but may be affected by society's views of their decision.

People on both sides of the abortion issue have formed opinions based on what they may believe to be scientific evidence. Sometimes the "evidence" is actually biased information or based on people's personal stories rather than scientific studies. Although there is no lack of information dedicated exclusively to the topic of abortion, the method of collecting the information, as well as its source, must be carefully considered, and the Internet should not automatically be trusted to provide accurate answers.

False Information

Many pro-life supporters are firmly convinced there are dramatic consequences to abortion. Pro-life websites and counseling centers generally offer long lists of possible side effects ranging from discomfort to bleeding to death. Many of the complications they mention can and do happen, but they are rare. The incidence of severe complications or death is small compared to the number of abortions performed annually. In fact, according to *TIME* magazine in 2012, research has shown that "women are actually 14 times more likely to die during or after [giving birth] than as a result of complications from abortion."[25]

Pro-choice advocates say one major source of misinformation is crisis pregnancy centers (CPCs), which are pro-life health care clinics. There are currently more CPCs in the United States than there are abortion clinics, and many pro-life people believe CPCs should receive funding instead of Planned Parenthood.

However, some CPCs use tactics that pro-choice people believe to be unethical or immoral. For instance, they may mislead women into thinking they are coming to an abortion clinic, and they often give women false information about reproductive health in an effort to scare them away from abortion. Some may also try to shame a woman into keeping her baby by implying that she would be a bad person if she had an abortion. Caitlin Bancroft, a writer for the *Huffington Post*, went to several CPCs in Virginia to see firsthand what they would say to her. She said, "Once inside, women are treated to a carefully crafted program of manipulation designed to dissuade them from choosing abortion, birth control, and if they're not married—sex."[26] Bancroft described her experience further:

> I could hear two employees whispering before entering my room, plotting strategies to reveal the test results and best manipulate my reaction. When they did finally clue me in, my concerns were casually brushed aside and used as ammunition for their agenda: I could care for a baby with no job, my parents would certainly help, and I could absolutely handle the stress. They even argued that I could be a law student while pregnant: "It will probably be good for the baby," the woman said, "because you will be sitting down all of the time."[27]

Some pro-life supporters defend CPCs, claiming it is actually abortion clinics, not CPCs, that lie to women. Many pro-life supporters believe CPCs are helpful and supportive of women who are unsure what to do about an unexpected pregnancy. In an article on the website of the American Center for Law and Justice (ACLJ), a nonprofit religious organization, one person wrote, "The CPCs I have worked with in my community provide licensed counseling services for both mothers and fathers, parenting classes, networks of babysitters, diapers, clothes, and post-partum [after-birth] care."[28] These items and resources are helpful to women who are considering abortion out of fear that they may not be able to take good care of their baby.

Some CPCs and other types of clinics may genuinely be helpful. For instance, All-Options Pregnancy Resource Center in

Bloomington, Indiana, is committed to giving women factual information about all their options so they can choose the best one for them. According to the website *Bustle*, "That means not only providing the typical goods of diapers, food, and baby clothes to new or expectant mothers, but also referring women to adoption agencies, parenting classes, medical providers, and abortion clinics. The pregnancy resource center [is] even establishing its own abortion fund for people who cannot afford the procedure or travel costs."[29] All-Options is not a CPC or an abortion clinic; it aims to give women neutral, accurate information about all their options so they can make the best choice for them.

However, although some CPCs and abortion clinics may be helpful, others have been proven to give women false information. Bancroft said that when she visited CPCs, she was told "the pill could cause breast cancer, that condoms are 'naturally porous' and don't protect against STIs, and that IUDs could kill me."[30] A yearlong investigation by NARAL found that 71 percent of CPCs in Virginia gave women false or misleading medical information similar to the information Bancroft was given. Abortion clinics are generally committed to giving women accurate information, but many states require women who are considering an abortion to undergo counseling before they can schedule the appointment, and sometimes the information doctors are required to give is false. As of 2015, 28 states require abortion clinics to "carry written informed consent brochures containing information about alternatives to abortion, the risks associated with abortion, and fetal development stages."[31] This information has often been found to be false or misleading; for example, some brochures state the risks of a procedure without mentioning that the chances of that risk happening are quite small. In 17 of those states, the doctor is only required to offer the brochure to patients, but in 11 states, the doctor is legally required to give it to the patient whether she wants it or not.

Many pro-life advocates approve of mandatory counseling because they believe it gives a woman as much information as possible before she makes her choice. On the other hand, many pro-choice advocates dislike it because they feel a woman has just as much right to choose whether she wants to be counseled as she does to choose whether she wants an abortion. Pro-choice advocates are especially critical of state-mandated counseling because the information is often medically inaccurate or written in a way that is intended to make a woman feel ashamed or afraid of her decision to have an abortion. For instance, some brochures "contain blatantly ideological language, referring to embryos as 'unborn children,' insisting that life begins at conception, and saying that abortion at any stage terminates the life of a separate, living being."[32] Receiving such brochures often does not change a woman's mind but may make her feel worse about her decision, which can lead to negative psychological effects afterward.

CPCs often offer a free pregnancy test to appeal to low-income women.

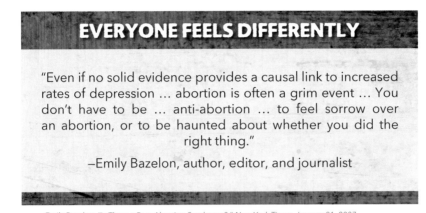

EVERYONE FEELS DIFFERENTLY

"Even if no solid evidence provides a causal link to increased rates of depression ... abortion is often a grim event ... You don't have to be ... anti-abortion ... to feel sorrow over an abortion, or to be haunted about whether you did the right thing."

—Emily Bazelon, author, editor, and journalist

Emily Bazelon, "Is There a Post-Abortion Syndrome?," *New York Times*, January 21, 2007. www.nytimes.com/2007/01/21/magazine/21abortion.t.html?pagewanted=3.

Is There a Risk of Breast Cancer?

Many pro-life supporters believe abortion causes abrupt hormonal changes that can lead to breast cancer later in life, and many CPCs tell their patients this. Over the years, studies of women with breast cancer seemed to indicate a higher incidence of prior abortion in these women. However, because the samples in the studies only included women with cancer, researchers were unable to select random samples to minimize false results.

In order to produce more reliable results, it would be necessary to determine the incidence of prior abortions among the same number of women without breast cancer. However, some researchers have suggested women who are healthy are less likely to reveal a previous abortion. This could make it appear as though women who have had an abortion have a higher incidence of breast cancer, even though the frequency between the two groups may actually be the same.

Beginning in the mid-1990s, results from more reliable studies became available for the first time. A Danish study completed in 1997 included every Danish woman born between April 1935 and March 1978—about 1.5 million women. Because the studies took the women's entire medical history into account, the results were considered more reliable. Researchers found no direct link between induced abortion and breast cancer. They did find a slightly increased risk for those who had late-term abortions, but cautioned the numbers involved were too small to be significant. Further study of late-term abortions is needed to verify or disprove any relationship between the two.

Since the publication of the Danish study, additional research has served to support its results. The Collaborative Group on Hormonal Factors in Breast Cancer, established in 1992, collects data from studies around the world for evaluation. In 2004, the Collaborative Group on Hormonal Factors in Breast Cancer evaluated the information in 53 separate studies, including 83,000 women from 16 countries that allow abortion. They reported no increase in a woman's risk of breast cancer due to miscarriage or induced abortion. As of 2014, according to the American Cancer Society, "scientific research studies have not found a cause-and-effect relationship between abortion and breast cancer."[33]

The American Cancer Society has declared, based on numerous studies, that it is a myth that abortion causes breast cancer.

Fear for Future Pregnancies

Some women who have an abortion do so because they do not want a baby at that particular time but do want a baby in the future. Because of this, many women are concerned with how an abortion will affect their ability to conceive a baby or carry it to term. Most researchers agree today's abortion procedures carry little risk of causing damage that would lead to infertility or miscarriage. Generally, abortions in the first trimester are nonsurgical procedures; rather than requiring cervical dilation or the scraping of the uterus to remove traces of pregnancy tissue, a woman simply takes medication.

The later an abortion is performed, the more intrusive it is for a woman's body. Any procedure that dilates the cervix can weaken it. In addition, the cleaning of the uterus can cause scarring. Multiple abortions tend to increase these factors, which can lead to the inability to carry a pregnancy to term in later attempts. However, as *Self* magazine pointed out, scarring can also occur when a woman gives birth, especially if she has multiple C-sections. In order to minimize the possibility of infertility, a woman who wishes to become pregnant after having one or more abortions should consult with her physician, who can determine whether scarring is a potential problem. According to *Self*, "In the 'very uncommon' cases where this becomes a problem, surgical removal of the scar tissue can usually solve the problem and restore fertility."[34] As long as an abortion is performed by a competent physician in a reputable hospital or clinic, the chances of being left infertile or miscarrying a future pregnancy are very low.

A trusted doctor can help a woman determine if having an abortion will affect her chances of having a baby in the future.

How Much Does an Abortion Cost?

Getting an abortion often requires careful financial planning. The price of an abortion varies depending on whether or not a person has insurance, whether or not the laws in their state allow their private insurance or Medicaid to cover an abortion, how late in the pregnancy the abortion takes place, and other factors. There are also extra costs that people may not know about. The *Daily Dot* explained,

> *According to the Guttmacher Institute ... over 53 percent of abortion patients decide to pay out of pocket, even if they are covered by Medicaid or a private insurance company. Though there are currently 15 states that cover abortion under Medicaid, even if you live in these states, some circumstances may prevent you from using your insurance. For example, in Iowa, the governor must approve all abortions paid for by Medicaid ...*

> *While abortion costs vary from state to state, the national average for a surgical abortion in the first trimester is around $500. Rates increase depending on how far along you are and can get up to $2,000 during the second trimester ... For many women, the actual procedure isn't the only large expense. Rebecca Wind, the associate director of communications at the Guttmacher Institute, says, "In 25 states, more than half of the women live in a county without an abortion provider." ...*

> *For women that live in those counties, travel and lodging can cost up to a few thousand dollars, plus there is the loss of pay for being out of work. However, even women who do have access to instate abortions but who aren't telling their family or housemates about the procedure still need a safe and comforting place to stay for recovery. Recovering from a medical abortion normally takes two or three days and requires a lot of heavy-duty maxi pads with wings, which surprisingly can cost you up to $100. Prescribed pain medication can range from $50-$80.[1]*

1. Rajaa Elidrissi, "The Financial Costs of an Uninsured Abortion," *Daily Dot*, updated May 19, 2017. www.dailydot.com/irl/how-much-does-an-abortion-cost/.

IS THERE LONG-TERM RISK?

"Most women do not experience psychological problems or regret their abortion 2 years post abortion, but some do. Those who do tend to be women with a prior history of ... depression ... Thus, for most women, elective abortion of an unintended pregnancy does not pose a risk to mental health."

–Brenda Major, professor of psychology

Brenda Major et al., "Psychological Responses of Women After First-Trimester Abortions," *Archives of General Psychiatry*, August 2000. www.archpsy.ama-assn.org/cgi/content/full/57/8/777.

The Risk of Complications

Because abortion is a medical procedure, there is always a chance of complications. However, many medical professionals agree that abortion has fewer potential complications than pregnancy or giving birth. Compared with being pregnant for a full nine months and the physical toll that pregnancy and childbirth can take on a woman's body—especially the body of a teenager—abortion is sometimes even considered a preferable option, at least in terms of physical health. Although this may be true in some cases, this is a decision a woman should make after consulting with her doctor.

According to the American Pregnancy Association, serious complications such as infection, scarring, heavy bleeding, and damage to the uterus or cervix occur in fewer than 1 out of 100 first trimester abortions and in about 1 out of 50 late-term abortions. The Association said, "It is important to understand that these risks are rare and that some of these risks are associated with child birth."[35]

The most common side effects resulting from an abortion include abdominal pain, nausea, vomiting, bleeding, and diarrhea. These may last for two to four weeks after the procedure.

Some women may experience no negative side effects at all after having an abortion. However, if a woman experiences any of the following symptoms, she should go to the hospital immediately:

- *Severe abdominal and back pain that prohibits you from standing up*

- *Bleeding that is heavier than a normal menstrual period*

- *Foul-smelling discharge*

- *Fever about 100.4 [degrees Fahrenheit]*

- *Continuing symptoms of pregnancy*[36]

WILLING TO LISTEN

"I politically identify as pro-choice, but I believe in the pro-voice model, which allows for different opinions on these issues. If [a protestor] ever gave me a chance to talk to her rather than just barking at me every time I enter the clinic, I'd want to know her story and why she is so committed to this kind of work."

—Natalia, abortion recipient

Quoted in Liz Welch, "6 Women on Their Terrifying, Infuriating Encounters with Abortion Clinic Protestors," *Cosmopolitan*, February 21, 2014. www.cosmopolitan.com/politics/news/a5669/abortion-clinic-protesters/.

The Psychological Impact

The decision to have an abortion is often not an easy one. Any unplanned pregnancy and the circumstances accompanying it put a woman under tremendous stress. During this stressful and complicated time, she must make a decision that has the potential to affect the rest of her life—and she must make it quickly, before it is too late for her to have an abortion according to state law. Her choices are limited: carry the baby to term and take on the responsibility of raising a child, carry the baby to term and place it for adoption, or have an abortion. Once a woman makes a decision, she must be willing to live with it. There is no going back. For some women, abortion is an easy and obvious choice, but others want time to think about it.

For some women, the emotional aspects of abortion linger long after the procedure is done. Post-abortion stress syndrome (PASS) is rare but can be a serious problem for women who are haunted by their decision. It mainly affects women who were pressured into an abortion they did not want, those who believed at the time of the abortion they were ending the life of a human being, or those who changed their beliefs about abortion after the fact. While the occurrence of PASS is statistically very low, women who fall into one of these categories may experience debilitating bouts of depression, anxiety, drug abuse, or suicidal episodes months or even years after their abortion. They may also

Secrecy Leads to Shame

Many pro-choice advocates are committed to breaking the stigma surrounding abortion because the feeling that they have done something shameful they must never speak of greatly increases the risk of an abortion recipient having negative psychological effects. According to a research paper published in 2011 in *Women's Health Issues*,

> Recent research indicates that two out of three women having abortions anticipate stigma if others were to learn about it; 58% felt they needed to keep their abortion secret from friends and family … the more a woman perceived others were looking down on her for having an abortion, the more she felt a need to keep the abortion secret. More than two thirds of women talked about their abortions "only a little bit" or "not at all." … the more women experienced stigma, the more likely they were to have adverse [negative] emotional outcomes … Social support that women receive from their immediate social networks, particularly their partners, mitigates [lessens] the effects of abortion stigma.[1]

The paper also mentioned that feelings of shame regarding abortions are not always constant; for example, a woman may feel fine about her decision until she encounters someone close to her who disapproves of abortion.

1. Alison Norris et al., "Abortion Stigma: A Reconceptualization of Constituents, Causes, and Consequences," *Women's Health Issues*, February 12, 2011. www.guttmacher.org/sites/default/files/pdfs/pubs/journals/Abortion-Stigma.pdf.

experience anger, guilt, shame, regret, isolation, or nightmares. Some pro-choice advocates accuse pro-life advocates of inventing PASS to convince women not to get an abortion because it is not a disorder that is recognized by the American Psychiatric Association. However, many mental health experts acknowledge that it is real, although it may simply be a form of post-traumatic stress disorder (PTSD). According to Dr. Susanne Babbel, "any event that causes trauma can indeed result in PTSD, and abortion is no exception."[37]

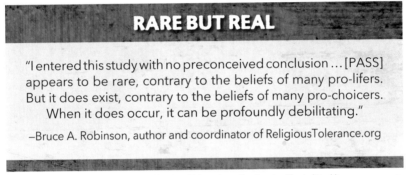

RARE BUT REAL

"I entered this study with no preconceived conclusion ... [PASS] appears to be rare, contrary to the beliefs of many pro-lifers. But it does exist, contrary to the beliefs of many pro-choicers. When it does occur, it can be profoundly debilitating."

–Bruce A. Robinson, author and coordinator of ReligiousTolerance.org

Bruce A. Robinson, "Overview: Do Abortions Trigger Later Emotional or Physical Health Problems?," ReligiousTolerance.org. www.religioustolerance.org/abohealth.htm.

In 1987, surgeon general C. Everett Koop was directed by President Ronald Reagan to prepare a report on the health effects of abortion. Koop, a vocal abortion opponent, gave the matter careful study over a 15-month period. Ultimately, he concluded the psychological effects of abortion to be minuscule from a public health perspective. In his report, Koop also noted the lack of scientifically sound research to make a direct connection between abortion and mental health. Psychological problems after an abortion may or may not be a result of the abortion. They may, instead, happen because of the factors surrounding the unintended pregnancy or because the woman had depression, anxiety, or some other mental disorder before she became pregnant. Either way, Koop noted, "obstetricians and gynecologists had long since concluded that the physical sequelae [aftereffects] of abortion were no different than those found in women who carried pregnancy to term or who had never been pregnant."[38]

There is no right or wrong way to feel after an abortion. Some women do not experience negative emotional effects, but others do.

Despite Koop's findings and subsequent studies that support them, pro-life supporters believe PASS is a common and frequently occurring side effect of abortion. Some organizations cite a frequency of PASS symptoms as high as 60 percent.

Although PASS is statistically rare, in 2005, the results of a five-year study by the University of Oslo in Norway showed negative psychological effects associated with abortion existed five years after the procedure for 1 out of 5 women. The study included 80 women who had abortions and 40 who had suffered miscarriages. The women were given several questionnaires 10 days, 6 months, 2 years, and 5 years after the event. At the 10-day point, 48 percent of the women who had miscarriages were suffering distress, while only 30 percent of those who had aborted indicated any emotional trauma. By the end of the 5 years, however, only 2.6 percent of the women who had suffered miscarriage were still showing signs of distress, compared to 20 percent of those who had an abortion.

Many pro-choice advocates do not believe PASS exists, or if they do, they believe the effects of PASS to be minimal. The Guttmacher Institute stated in 2006, "It is fair to say that neither the weight of the scientific evidence to date nor the observable reality of 33 years of legal abortion in the United States comports with the idea that having an abortion is any more dangerous to a woman's long-term mental health than delivering and parenting a child that she did not intend to have or placing a baby for adoption."[39] Many women report feeling a sense of relief after they have an abortion, knowing they will not have to raise a child they are not ready for.

What Happens Next?

The debate over abortion will likely never be completely settled. In many cases, a matter is mostly settled once a law is passed, but this situation is different. Abortion has been legal in the United States for nearly half a century, and for that entire time, pro-life advocates have fought to make it illegal again. If they eventually succeed, pro-choice advocates will certainly fight to make it legal again. State governments are constantly proposing new laws, many of which restrict abortion access, so it is difficult to say exactly what will happen in the future. However, it is possible to make some guesses.

Changing Trends in the Pro-Life Movement

The pro-life movement has historically been seen as very religious and dominated by older white men. However, in recent years, young, secular (non-religious) Millennial women have stepped forward to create pro-life organizations. Many of these organizations are committed to preventing not just abortion, but all forms of violence—a view that sometimes differs from the pro-life views of the past, when some groups were accused of not caring about helping a person after they were born. Many secular Millennial pro-life activists are concerned about human rights and generally support issues such as LGBT+ rights, Black Lives Matter, anti-human trafficking laws, and an end to the death penalty.

Selective Abortion

In some countries where boys are valued more highly than girls, women may have an abortion if they find out their child is female. Several states have passed laws against this kind of selective abortion, and several others have proposed similar laws. Lawmakers have been criticized by some groups of unfairly targeting Asian American and Pacific Islander (AAPI) women because of stereotypes that daughters are never wanted in Asian families. In an opinion article for *The Hill*, Mohini Lal, an Indian woman, explained how this happens:

> In six states, most recently Arkansas, lawmakers have passed sex-selective abortion bans. These bans often mandate that doctors not only ask their patients if they're having an abortion in order to have a child of a specific gender, but some even demand doctors search a patient's medical history or give patients' medical histories to local law enforcement in order to look for evidence of son preference.
>
> The state legislators who bring these bills say that they are trying to guard against immigrants who bring backwards values from their home countries. Specifically, they are trying to guard against the values they think my family and families like mine brought with us. By relying on racist stereotypes about AAPI families, anti-choice lawmakers use language about gender discrimination to limit all of our abortion rights.[40]

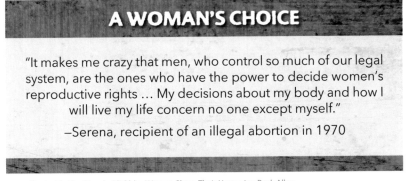

A WOMAN'S CHOICE

"It makes me crazy that men, who control so much of our legal system, are the ones who have the power to decide women's reproductive rights ... My decisions about my body and how I will live my life concern no one except myself."

—Serena, recipient of an illegal abortion in 1970

Quoted in Lisa Woods, "9 Older Women Share Their Harrowing Back Alley Abortion Stories," *Thought Catalog*, December 30, 2015. thoughtcatalog.com/lisa-woods/2015/12/9-older-women-share-their-harrowing-back-alley-abortion-stories/.

If an American woman chooses to have an abortion after finding out the results of her baby's tests, it is more often because the fetus has some kind of genetic problem. Some of these disorders are generally fatal, such as Tay-Sachs disease, a rare, incurable genetic disorder that often kills children before they turn four. Others are not, such as Down syndrome and autism.

The ethics of selective abortion are hotly debated, even more so than abortions that are performed because a woman does not feel ready to raise a child. Even some pro-choice people feel sex-selective and disability-selective abortions are wrong. The availability of prenatal genetic testing is changing the kinds of

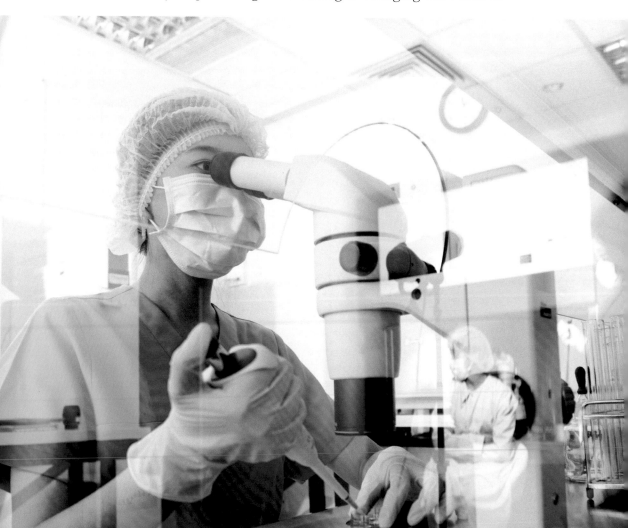

questions being raised by the abortion issue. The idea of being able to choose which fetuses are healthy enough or "perfect" enough to be born is a subject no one seems ready to tackle just yet. Many argue that the best way to prevent these kinds of abortions is not to pass a law—especially since women are not required to tell the doctor why they are getting an abortion, so it would be hard to enforce—but rather to change society's attitudes regarding women and people with disabilities. If people do not view either of these groups as undesirable, experts say, there will be no reason to abort a child that falls into one of those categories.

Some people worry that advancements in genetic research and prenatal testing will lead to a higher rate of selective abortions.

A Futuristic Invention

Another possible agent of change in the abortion debate is the science of ectogenesis (the creation of life outside the uterus). Advancements in this field have the potential to change the point at which a fetus becomes viable to a much earlier stage of pregnancy. This might one day be possible through the development of artificial wombs. The success of this work could dramatically impact abortions in the future.

In April 2017, scientists at the Children's Hospital of Philadelphia announced that they had used an artificial womb to gestate a lamb fetus for four weeks. The womb looked like a large plastic bag full of a liquid similar to amniotic fluid, with attachments so the lamb could be fed nutrients.

Researchers at the Children's Hospital of Philadelphia (shown here) hope their artificial womb will help keep premature babies alive, but some people believe it could be used to keep an aborted fetus alive as well.

Some pro-life supporters have seized on the idea of artificial wombs as a possible solution to the problem of unintended pregnancies. Since most states already have restrictions on abortion after viability, they see the development of this technology as a way to extend the period of viability. Some think this is a good way to end the abortion debate because a woman will be able to have the fetus removed from her womb without killing it, therefore making both sides happy. However, this raises other questions. Who will take care of the baby after it is viable? How much will it cost to provide an artificial womb to each unintended child? Would scientists be able to remove a zygote from a woman's body or would she be required to carry the child until it becomes a fetus? The research team "insists it is not looking to replace mothers or extend the limits of viability—merely to find a better way to support babies who are born too early,"[41] so using an artificial womb to end the abortion debate may never become a reality.

The Facts About Neonaticide

Many people have heard horror stories about neonaticide—the killing of a newborn within the first few hours of life. Some people believe this is a form of abortion supported by pro-choice advocates, and stories about women giving birth and throwing their child in a trash can are sometimes circulated by pro-life advocates who believe their pro-choice opponents support this. However, the truth is that even pro-choice advocates view killing a child after it is born as murder. Neonaticide is rarely committed—it accounts for only about 2 to 3 percent of all homicides—and when it happens, it is generally because a young woman was so traumatized by her pregnancy that she did not know how to deal with it. When she gives birth, a teen who is in denial may panic at the reality of the baby and harm or abandon it without thinking of consequences. Most regret their decision after they have time to think about it. Neonaticide is not and has never been an approved form of abortion.

Finding Solutions

A more practical solution to the abortion debate may hinge on finding common ground. Most pro-life and pro-choice advocates can agree the root cause of abortion is unintended or unviable pregnancy. Even some pro-choice supporters do not feel abortion is a good solution. By working together to increase the range of possible solutions, it may be possible to dramatically reduce the number of unintended pregnancies that end in abortion.

In the 1990s, an organization called the Common Ground Network for Life and Choice made an effort to identify areas of overlapping concern to both sides of the abortion debate. Some of their discussions focused on preventing teen pregnancy, making adoption a more accessible choice, and increasing options for women. The Common Ground approach encouraged pro-life and pro-choice supporters to spend less time engaged in debate and more time combining their efforts to achieve shared goals. By the late 1990s, however, the lack of public focus on the abortion question along with the loss of most of their funding brought an end to the group. In spite of this, their goal of focusing on shared concerns and common ground is a worthwhile approach for the future.

USING THE POWER OF THE INTERNET

"Perhaps it's time to fully embrace the power of 21st century communication and direct it toward public health goals more deliberately ... Online material and social media could help to fill the gaps in sex education and support for many young people."

–Victor Strasburger, adolescent medical expert, and Sarah Brown, CEO of The National Campaign to Prevent Teen and Unplanned Pregnancy

Quoted in Alexandra Sifferlin, "Why Schools Can't Teach Sex Ed," *TIME*, accessed July 19, 2017. time.com/why-schools-cant-teach-sex-ed/.

Teaching Safe Sex

One of the areas identified by both pro-life and pro-choice groups as common ground is the need for better sex education. A few years ago, efforts to introduce comprehensive sex education in schools were met with resistance, but polls show a shift in attitude. Today, the majority of Americans agree sex education should be taught in schools.

While almost everyone agrees school sex education programs are a good idea, how far this education should go is still a topic of debate. Some parents favor an abstinence-only or abstinence-plus approach. Abstinence-only means teaching young adults that abstinence—not having sex—is the only correct choice; these programs do not cover issues such as contraception or consent, and many use scare tactics and false or misleading information to try to make teens afraid to have sex. Currently, "only 22 states mandate sex education, and only 13 require the information to be 'medically accurate.'"[42] Abstinence-plus means teaching teens that abstinence is best, but it includes information about condoms, contraception, and making responsible decisions about sex.

Many pro-choice advocates favor comprehensive sex education, which also includes information about family planning, reproduction, body image, sexual values, dating and relationships, communication and negotiation skills, and how to avoid STDs, in addition to basic contraception. Polls have shown that this type of sex education is most popular with teens, who want to learn more about their bodies and how to navigate relationships and sex. When asked, teens have suggested less emphasis on anatomy and scare tactics and more discussion of negotiation in sexual relationships, as well as basic communication skills. They also suggest that information about health clinics should be highly visible in places young people often go to, such as shopping centers, school restrooms, and movie theaters.

Current research shows failure to address teen sexuality leads to higher incidences of STDs and teenage pregnancy. In countries where comprehensive sex education programs are in place, the rates are much lower. The 2015 teen pregnancy rate in the

United States, for example, was about 21 per 1,000 women ages 15 to 19, compared with 4 per 1,000 in the Netherlands, where more comprehensive sex education programs are the norm.

However, many people oppose comprehensive sex education programs on religious grounds, saying they encourage

teens to have sex, which some people believe is immoral. Many pro-life advocates also fear this will lead to increased teen pregnancy and abortion rates, despite statistics that clearly show the opposite. In 2007, the results of a nine-year study commissioned by Congress and conducted by Mathematica Policy Research

Multiple research projects have shown that comprehensive sex education classes are more effective than abstinence-only or abstinence-plus programs at preventing unintended pregnancies, reducing the rate of abortions and STDs, and encouraging healthy relationships among teenagers.

showed abstinence-only programs were no more likely to influence teens to delay sexual initiation than their comprehensive counterparts and may actually increase unplanned pregnancies because students taking abstinence-only classes are less likely to use contraception consistently or correctly. Another study in 2008 by the University of Washington found that "teenagers who received comprehensive sex education were 60 percent less likely to get pregnant than [those] who received abstinence-only education,"[43] and a 2011 study published in the journal *PLOS One* found similar results. States with the highest teen pregnancy rates are those that teach abstinence-only education.

WHEN IS ABORTION A RACIAL ISSUE?

"If you're a person who's saying, 'I care about black babies in the womb,' and then you see Tamir Rice, you see Mike Brown [who were both killed], and your first response is that the black community doesn't really care because they're aborting all their babies—if that's your first response, then something is missing ... You're not showing empathy."

–Christina Bennett, African American pro-life activist

Quoted in Ruth Graham, "The New Culture of Life," *Slate*, October 11, 2016. www.slate.com/articles/double_x/cover_story/2016/10/the_future_of_the_pro_life_movement.html.

Additionally, many young adults are exposed early on to sexual content through social media, movies, TV shows, and music. If they receive abstinence-only or abstinence-plus sex education and their parents or guardians do not have a discussion with them to help fill in the gaps, they may be confused about many things, including what informed consent is and how to discuss it with a partner, what to do if they or a friend is gay, and how to recognize when a relationship is abusive. Girls are often taught how to say no to sex and how to protect themselves, but boys are generally not taught that they have a responsibility to ask permission before attempting any kind of sexual contact. Experts say that treating boys as if they are not in control of their own actions causes many young men to stop paying attention in sex education classes, so they may miss important information.

Better sex education programs are a common goal for most pro-life and pro-choice groups—when they can reach agreement about the content. As efforts are made to work together to create more effective programs, many people on both sides hope to reduce the number of unintended pregnancies and ultimately the number of abortions.

The Impact of Legislation

States are continuously introducing new laws, and it is difficult to know what the next one will be. Advocates for each side propose laws for the cause they support and fight against laws proposed by the opposite side. Each side wins some battles and loses others. In May 2017, for instance, Texas passed a law banning D&E, the most common type of procedure performed in second-trimester abortions. The law stated that any doctor found to be performing the operation would face felony charges, which would have them facing severe jail sentences. On the other hand, a 2016 law was struck down in Oklahoma; the law stated that abortion providers would be required to "take samples of fetal tissue from patients younger than 14 and preserve them for state investigators. The law also set new criminal penalties for providers who violate abortion-related statutes [laws] as well as individuals who help a minor evade the requirement to obtain parental consent."[44]

The election of Donald Trump as president has also had an impact on the abortion debate. Trump stated during the 2016 debates that he is pro-life and would like to see *Roe v. Wade* overturned and the decision left up to individual states. Based on the number of restrictions many states have passed, a large number of states would likely make abortion illegal if *Roe v. Wade* was overturned. When asked about whether he would defund Planned Parenthood, Trump said, "I would defund it because of the abortion factor, which they say is 3 percent. I don't know what percentage it is … But I would defund it, because I'm pro-life. But millions of women are helped by Planned Parenthood."[45] Because of this conflicting view, Trump offered

Planned Parenthood a deal in March 2017: "Stop doing abortions and you can keep the federal funding that the House Republican bill to replace Obamacare would otherwise eliminate,"[46] as Emily Bazelon summarized in the *New York Times*. Since this law would be very restrictive and federal funds are not used for abortions anyway, Planned Parenthood rejected the proposal. As of September 2017, it is unclear what Trump's next step on this issue will be.

Laws regarding abortion are frequently debated in Congress. Donald Trump has announced that he does not support abortion, but it is uncertain what laws he will propose on this issue.

In response to Trump's statements during his presidential campaign, a large women's march was held in Washington, D.C., in January 2017. Smaller marches were held in cities across the country. The marches protested not just anti-abortion laws, but other issues of sexism, including sexual harassment and unequal pay. Protests of various sizes continue to be held every time a new anti-abortion law is proposed, but the effect of these protests remains to be seen.

As the 21st century unfolds, the abortion debate that has been raging for nearly 50 years seems destined to continue. The questions coming out of this debate have polarized the nation and created two very different schools of thought. Both sides are committed to fighting for their cause; only time will tell which group will win or whether a compromise is possible.

Chapter 1: A Debate About Morality

1. Quoted in "When Does Life Begin,"
    AllAboutPopularIssues.org, accessed July 20, 2017.
    www.allaboutpopularissues.org/when-does-life-begin-faq.
    htm.

2. Quoted in Adrienne Lafrance, "Clinton's Unapologetic
    Defense of Abortion Rights," *The Atlantic*, October 20,
    2016. www.theatlantic.com/health/archive/2016/10/hillary-
    clintons-powerful-defense-of-abortion-rights/504866/.

3. "First Lady Hillary Rodham Clinton Remarks at NARAL
    Anniversary Luncheon Washington, D.C., January
    22, 1999," WhiteHouse.gov, accessed July 20, 2017.
    clintonwhitehouse3.archives.gov/WH/EOP/First_Lady/
    html/generalspeeches/1999/19990122.html.

4. Quoted in Lafrance, "Clinton's Unapologetic Defense."

5. George Monbiot, "Face Facts, Cardinal. Our Awful
    Rate of Abortion Is Partly Your Responsibility," *The
    Guardian*, February 26, 2008. www.theguardian.com/
    commentisfree/2008/feb/26/health.religion.

6. Quoted in Alan Levinovitz, "Why Do Pro-Life Activists
    Seem Only to Care About Unborn Lives?," *Slate*, January
    27, 2017. www.slate.com/blogs/xx_factor/2017/01/27/
    the_flaw_in_the_pro_life_argument_that_i_can_t_
    ignore.html.

7. Sarah Zhang, "Why Science Can't Say When a Baby's
    Life Begins," *Wired*, October 2, 2015. www.wired.
    com/2015/10/science-cant-say-babys-life-begins/.

8. C. Everett Koop and Timothy Johnson, *Let's Talk: An Honest Conversation on Critical Issues: Abortion, Euthanasia, AIDS, Health Care*. Grand Rapids, MI: Zondervan, 1992, p. 21.

9. Anna Quindlen, *Living Out Loud*. New York, NY: Random House, 1988, p. 210.

Chapter 2: The Debate over Government Involvement

10. James Wilson, *Of the Natural Rights of Individuals*, TeachingAmericanHistory.org, accessed July 20, 2017. teachingamericanhistory.org/library/document/of-the-natural-rights-of-individuals/.

11. Quoted in Lisa Woods, "9 Older Women Share Their Harrowing Back Alley Abortion Stories," *Thought Catalog*, December 20, 2015. thoughtcatalog.com/lisa-woods/2015/12/9-older-women-share-their-harrowing-back-alley-abortion-stories/.

12. Margaret Talbot, "The Supreme Court's Just Application of the Undue-Burden Standard for Abortion," *The New Yorker*, June 27, 2016. www.newyorker.com/news/news-desk/the-supreme-courts-just-application-of-the-undue-burden-standard-for-abortion.

13. Quoted in Newsmax Wires, "Anti-Abortion Laws Lead to Clinic Shutdowns Nationwide," *Newsmax*, August 27, 2013. www.newsmax.com/Newsfront/abortion-clinics-republicans-restrictions/2013/08/27/id/522437/.

14. Gina Pollack, "What It's Like to Endure a Forced Waiting Period Before Your Abortion," *Broadly*, April 26, 2016. broadly.vice.com/en_us/article/qkg753/what-its-like-to-endure-a-forced-waiting-period-before-your-abortion.

15. Quoted in Newsmax Wires, "Anti-Abortion Laws Lead to Clinic Shutdowns Nationwide."

16. Ronald Reagan, *Abortion and the Conscience of the Nation*. New York, NY: Thomas Nelson, Human Life Foundation, 1984, p. 16.

17. "An Overview of Abortion in the United States," Guttmacher Institute. www.guttmacher.org/media/presskits/2005/06/28/abortionoverview.html.

Chapter 3: Ethical Dilemmas

18. Quoted in Tara Haelle, "No, Late-Term Abortions Don't 'Rip' Babies Out of Wombs—and They Exist for a Reason," *Forbes*, October 20, 2016. www.forbes.com/sites/tarahaelle/2016/10/20/no-late-term-abortions-dont-rip-babies-out-of-wombs-but-they-are-needed/#94166315cf8e.

19. Quoted in Jia Tolentino, "Interview with a Woman Who Recently Had an Abortion at 32 Weeks," Jezebel, June 15, 2016. jezebel.com/interview-with-a-woman-who-recently-had-an-abortion-at-1781972395.

20. Keri J. Dodd, "School Condom Availability," Advocates for Youth, February 1998. www.advocatesforyouth.org/publications/449-school-condom-availability.

21. Joerg Dreweke, "New Clarity for the U.S. Abortion Debate: A Steep Drop in Unintended Pregnancy Is Driving Recent Abortion Declines," Guttmacher Institute, March 18, 2016. www.guttmacher.org/gpr/2016/03/new-clarity-us-abortion-debate-steep-drop-unintended-pregnancy-driving-recent-abortion.

22. Sarah Torre, "Congress Should End Federal Funding to Planned Parenthood and Redirect It Toward Other Health Care Options," The Heritage Foundation, September 22, 2015. www.heritage.org/health-care-reform/report/congress-should-end-federal-funding-planned-parenthood-and-redirect-it.

23. Sandhya Somashekhar, "Ohio Governor Vetoes 'Heartbeat Bill' but Signs Another Abortion Restriction into Law," *Washington Post*, December 13, 2016. www.washingtonpost.com/news/post-nation/wp/2016/12/13/ohio-governor-vetoes-heartbeat-bill-but-signs-into-law-another-abortion-restriction/?utm_term=.715ef05a0744.

24. Somashekhar, "Ohio Governor Vetoes 'Heartbeat Bill.'"

Chapter 4: Health Effects

25. Bonnie Rochman, "Why Abortion Is Less Risky than Childbirth," *TIME*, January 25, 2012. healthland.time.com/2012/01/25/why-abortion-is-less-risky-than-childbirth/.

26. Caitlin Bancroft, "What I Learned Undercover at a Crisis Pregnancy Center," *Huffington Post*, updated October 15, 2013. www.huffingtonpost.com/caitlin-bancroft/crisis-pregnancy-center_b_3763196.html.

27. Bancroft, "What I Learned Undercover at a Crisis Pregnancy Center."

28. "Cheap Shot at Crisis Pregnancy Centers Nothing More than Big Abortion Lies Cloaked in Bad Comedy," ACLJ, May 2016. aclj.org/pro-life/cheap-shot-at-crisis-pregnancy-centers-nothing-more-than-big-abortion-lies-cloaked-in-bad-comedy.

29. Lauren Barbato, "Indiana's All-Options Pregnancy Resource Center Finally Offers Women the 'Options' They Actually Need," *Bustle*, May 12, 2015. www.bustle.com/articles/79838-indianas-all-options-pregnancy-resource-center-finally-offers-women-the-options-they-actually-need.

30. Bancroft, "What I Learned Undercover at a Crisis Pregnancy Center."

31. Callie Beusman, "A State-by-State List of the Lies Abortion Doctors Are Forced to Tell Women," *Broadly*, August 18, 2016. broadly.vice.com/en_us/article/nz88gx/a-state-by-state-list-of-the-lies-abortion-doctors-are-forced-to-tell-women.

32. Beusman, "A State-by-State List of the Lies Abortion Doctors Are Forced to Tell Women."

33. American Cancer Society Medical and Editorial Content Team, "Abortion and Breast Cancer Risk," American Cancer Society, June 19, 2014. www.cancer.org/cancer/cancer-causes/medical-treatments/abortion-and-breast-cancer-risk.html.

34. Amy Marturana, "Does Having an Abortion Affect Your Future Fertility?," *Self*, August 31, 2016. www.self.com/story/does-having-an-abortion-affect-your-future-fertility.

35. "Possible Side Effects After Abortion," American Pregnancy Association, September 3, 2016. americanpregnancy.org/unplanned-pregnancy/abortion-side-effects/.

36. "Possible Side Effects After Abortion," American Pregnancy Association.

37. Susanne Babbel, "Post Abortion Stress Syndrom (PASS)—Does It Exist?," *Psychology Today*, October 25, 2010. www.psychologytoday.com/blog/somatic-psychology/201010/post-abortion-stress-syndrome-pass-does-it-exist.

38. Quoted in Heather D. Boonstra, Rachel Benson Gold, Cory L. Richards, and Lawrence B. Finer, *Abortion in Women's Lives*, Guttmacher Institute, 2006, p. 24. www.guttmacher.org/pubs/2006/05/04/AiWL.pdf.

39. Susan Cohen, "Abortion and Mental Health: Myths and Realities," Guttmacher Institute, August 1 2006. www.guttmacher.org/about/gpr/2006/08/abortion-and-mental-health-myths-and-realities.

Chapter 5: What Happens Next?

40. Mohini Lal, "Why Asian American Pacific Islander Families Don't Need Sex-Selective Abortion Bans," *The Hill*, May 13, 2017. thehill.com/blogs/pundits-blog/healthcare/333200-why-asian-american-pacific-islander-families-dont-need-sex.

41. Michelle Roberts, "Premature Lambs Kept Alive in 'Plastic Bag' Womb," BBC, April 25, 2017. www.bbc.com/news/health-39693851.

42. Quoted in Rachel Sanoff, "7 Problems With the State of Sex Ed in America Today, and How We Can Make It Better," *Bustle*, August 27, 2015. www.bustle.com/articles/104233-7-problems-with-the-state-of-sex-ed-in-america-today-and-how-we-can-make.

43. Matt Essert, "The States With the Highest Teenage Birth Rates Have One Thing in Common," Mic, September 15, 2014. mic.com/articles/98886/the-states-with-the-highest-teenage-birth-rates-have-one-thing-in-common#.HnpB30T59.

44. Joseph Ax, "Oklahoma Supreme Court Strikes Down Restrictive Abortion Law," Reuters, October 4, 2016. www.reuters.com/article/us-oklahoma-abortion-idUSKCN12420G.

45. "Donald Trump on Abortion," On the Issues, October 19, 2016. www.ontheissues.org/2016/Donald_Trump_Abortion.htm.

46. Emily Bazelon, "Trump's Abortion Strategy," *New York Times*, March 10, 2017. www.nytimes.com/2017/03/10/opinion/trumps-abortion-strategy.html.

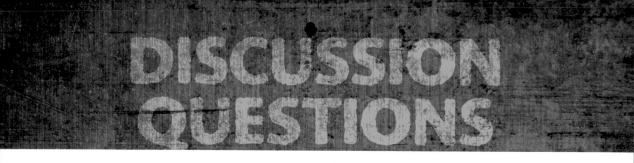

Chapter 1:
A Debate About Morality

1. What are some things you think are moral? What are some things you think are immoral?

2. Do you consider yourself pro-choice or pro-life?

3. Under what circumstances—if any—do you think abortion should be allowed?

Chapter 2:
The Debate over Government Involvement

1. Do you think abortion should be legal or illegal?

2. What are some of the dangers of a self-induced abortion?

3. Do you think abortion restrictions place an undue burden on women seeking an abortion?

Chapter 3:
Ethical Dilemmas

1. Do you think late-term abortions should be legal or illegal?

2. What type of sexual education program would you prefer to take: abstinence-only, abstinence-plus, or comprehensive?

3. Do you support government funding for Planned Parenthood?

Chapter 4:
Health Effects

1. What is your opinion of crisis pregnancy centers?

2. What are some complications that may result after an abortion?

3. What kinds of costs are associated with an abortion? Can you think of any that were not mentioned in the text?

Chapter 5:
What Happens Next?

1. If you were in charge, what kind of abortion laws would you pass?

2. Do you think men should be in charge of making abortion laws?

3. What is some common ground in the pro-choice and pro-life movements? Do you think it is possible to find a solution that will make most people happy?

Center Against Forced Abortions (CAFA)

(210) 614-7157

info@txjf.org

thejusticefoundation.org/cafa/

> Some women do not want to have an abortion, but feel pressured to do so by their parents, a partner, or someone else. Teenage girls face more pressure than older women. CAFA gives women who feel forced to have an abortion legal resources to turn to so they can fight the person or people pressuring them and make their own choice about their pregnancy.

NARAL Pro-Choice America

1156 15th St. NW, Suite 700

Washington, DC 20005

(202) 973-3000

www.prochoiceamerica.org

> NARAL Pro-Choice America is committed to protecting the right to choose and electing candidates who will promote policies to prevent unintended pregnancy.

New Wave Feminism

destiny@newwavefeminists.com

www.newwavefeminists.com

> This pro-life organization believes that rather than making abortion illegal, activists should work to change society so abortion becomes unnecessary. In their view, this means supporting programs that make it easier for a woman to keep her baby, such as paid maternity and paternity leave, as well as better access to birth control to prevent unplanned pregnancies. The organization is also anti-war, anti-death penalty, and anti-torture.

Planned Parenthood Federation of America

123 William Street, 10th Floor
New York, NY 10038
1-800-230-PLAN (1-800-230-7526)
www.plannedparenthood.org

Planned Parenthood provides health care services, sex education, and sexual health information to millions of women and men of all ages and sexual orientations. For more than 100 years, Planned Parenthood has promoted a common sense approach to health and well-being based on respect for each individual's right to make informed, independent decisions about sex, health, and family planning. Local clinic locations and contact information can be found on the main website.

Secular Pro-Life

info@secularprolife.org
www.secularprolife.org

Secular Pro-Life is aimed at young people who are not religious but oppose abortion as well as the death penalty and assisted suicide. The organization supports exceptions to abortion when the life of the mother or child is at stake.

Books

Feldt, Gloria. *Behind Every Choice Is a Story*. Denton, TX: University of North Texas Press, 2004.
> This book is a discussion of unplanned pregnancy options interwoven with personal stories.

Hand, Carol. *Abortion: Interpreting the Constitution*. New York, NY: Rosen Publishing Group, 2015.
> This book describes the shift in abortion laws over the years and discusses how pro-choice and pro-life groups have interpreted the Constitution.

Hayes, Leah. *Not Funny Ha-Ha: A Handbook for Something Hard*. Seattle, WA: Fantagraphics Books, 2015.
> This nonfiction graphic novel discusses two different women who go through two different types of abortions, letting readers know what to expect from the process.

Watkins, Christine, ed., *The Ethics of Abortion*. Detroit, MI: Greenhaven, 2005.
> This book is a collection of essays from both sides of the abortion debate related to ethics and morality.

Wittenstein, Vicki Oransky. *Reproductive Rights: Who Decides?* Minneapolis, MN: Twenty-First Century Books, 2016.
> Abortion has become a highly political issue, and laws are in place that either help or prevent a woman from getting an abortion. This book explains who makes the laws and why they decide to vote one way or another on a particular issue.

Websites

"Abortion Access: All Sides of the Issue"

www.religioustolerance.org/abortion.htm

This website lists as many of the various viewpoints about abortion as possible, including many pro-life beliefs and a diverse listing of pro-choice beliefs.

Exhale: After Abortion Support

exhaleprovoice.org/after-abortion-support

This website describes itself as "pro-voice," meaning it is neither pro-life nor pro-choice. It gives women who have had an abortion tips about how to find a therapist or support group and ideas for self-care, and it also lists ways to support a loved one who has had an abortion. There is also a toll-free, confidential talkline women and men can call to discuss their feelings about an abortion they or a loved one has had.

Guttmacher Institute

www.guttmacher.org

The Guttmacher Institute is known for its research in the field of reproductive health. Although pro-choice in philosophy, the data provided by the Guttmacher Institute is generally considered reliable by both pro-choice and pro-life organizations.

National Latina Institute for Reproductive Health

www.latinainstitute.org/en

Latina women are at a higher risk for unintended pregnancy than many other groups of women and are less likely to be able to afford an abortion. The Institute aims to help shape laws that affect abortion access and affordability, LGBT+ issues, access to contraception, issues concerning immigrant women, and more.

National Network of Abortion Funds

abortionfunds.org/about

> This organization helps low-income women pay for their abortions and gives a list of places they may be able to stay for free during the recovery period.

Scarleteen

www.scarleteen.com

> For teens who feel that their sex education classes are not answering all of their questions, Scarleteen has advice columns on topics such as birth control, sexual autonomy, creating a healthy relationship, issues that affect the LGBT+ community, and more. A live chat is available, and readers can submit their questions to the advice columnists.

SisterSong

sistersong.net/reproductive-justice/

> SisterSong is an organization that fights for reproductive justice for indigenous women, women of color, and LGBT+ people. Reproductive justice, in their view, includes not just the right to choose whether or not to have children, but also the right to have control over what happens to their own bodies and the ability to raise children in safe, sustainable communities.

ABOUT THE AUTHOR

Meghan Green has edited a number of books for young people on the topics of social justice and self-esteem. She also sometimes gives talks at local schools on these topics. She is a social worker who specializes in working with developmentally disabled individuals. Meghan lives in Pennsylvania with her husband, Kris.